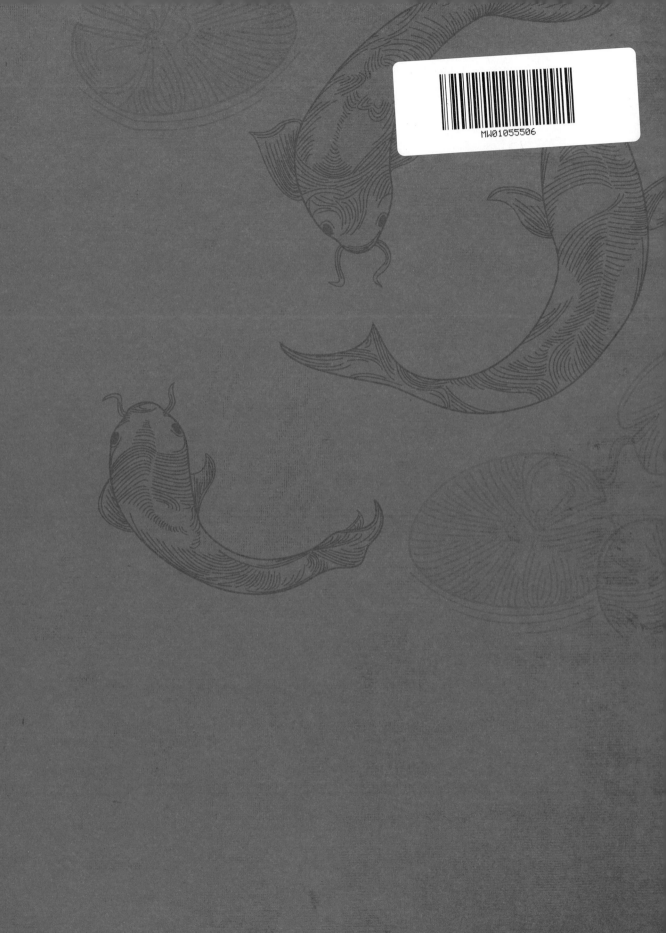

IN DEFENSE OF
OUR NEIGHBORS

THE WALT AND MILLY WOODWARD STORY

Sonoji Sakai surveyed his farm with daughter Kay in the final days before they and 225 other Bainbridge Islanders were removed from their community and incarcerated. Unlike many Island Nikkei who would lose their farms during the war, the Sakais were fortunate enough to have surrogates available to take care of the farm while they were away and the means to keep the payments up to date.

At the time of the evacuation of the Japanese Americans in March of 1942, Bainbridge Island had two active ferry terminals. The Winslow Dock, seen here guarded by United States Army soldiers on the day of the evacuation, was the main terminal. The Japanese Americans were transported off the Island from Eagledale Dock, located across Eagle Harbor from the Winslow Dock.

IN DEFENSE OF
OUR NEIGHBORS

THE WALT AND MILLY WOODWARD STORY

MARY WOODWARD

FOREWORD BY DAVID GUTERSON

FENWICK

Sixty-six years after the exclusion, the site of the old Eagledale Dock is being transformed into a memorial honoring the evacuated Island Japanese Americans and their friends and neighbors who defended them. Here, Earl Hanson (right), who watched as his Japanese American friends were loaded onto the awaiting ferry, and Kay Nakao and Shig Moritani, both former exiles, recall the sad day.

This book is dedicated to Kay Nakao and Paul Ohtaki, whom I love as family.

It is presented in memory of my beloved Donald and Jerry Nakata, a treasured friend.

I offer this book, with grateful respect for my parents' example, to my sons Brodie and Riley Woodward-Pratt and my friend Eddie Nakata and the others of their generation and generations to follow.

—Mary Woodward, March 2008

Fenwick Publishing Group, Inc.
3147 Point White Drive, Suite 100
Bainbridge Island, Washington 98110

Fenwick Publishing produces, publishes, and markets custom publications for corporations, institutions, nonprofit organizations, and individuals.

www.fenwickpublishing.com

President and Publisher: Timothy J. Connolly
Vice President, Development: Sarah Morgans
Editorial and Production Assistant: Patrick R. Duff
Designer: Kevin Berger
Manuscript Editor: Bill Thorness
Copy Editor: Betsy Holt
Proofreader: Lisa Wolff
Indexer: Ken DellaPenta

Bainbridge Island Japanese American Community
1298 Grow Avenue NW
Bainbridge Island, Washington 98110

First edition
Printed in China

17 16 15 14 13 12 11 10 09 08 1 2 3 4 5

ISBN: 978-0-9749510-7-2

Library of Congress Cataloging-in-Publication Data

Woodward, Mary, 1946–
  In defense of our neighbors : the Walt and Milly
  Woodward story / Mary Woodward. —1st ed.
    p. cm.
  Includes bibliographical references and index.
  ISBN 978-0-9749510-7-2
1. Japanese Americans—Evacuation and relocation, 1942–1945. 2. Japanese Americans—Evacuation and relocation, 1942–1945—Press coverage—Washington—Bainbridge Island. 3. World War, 1939–1945—Japanese Americans. 4. Japanese Americans—Washington—Bainbridge Island—History. 5. Woodward, Milly, 1909–1989. 6. Woodward, Walt, 1910–2001. 7. Bainbridge Review.
I. Title.
  D769.8.A6W662008
  940.53'14730922—dc22
                              2008014667

Table of Contents

Walt and Milly Woodward argued against the exclusion in the Bainbridge Review, *the newspaper they published. Throughout the exclusion, they used this forum to defend the rights of Japanese Americans such as Fumiko Hayashida and her daughter, Kayo, seen here waiting at Eagledale Dock. The tags worn by the pair were similar to the ones worn by all the evacuees during their transfer to Manzanar.*

Full disclosure: My name is mentioned favorably toward the end of the book, as is my novel *Snow Falling on Cedars*, for which I'm grateful to Mary Woodward. On the other hand, I hope you'll believe that I wanted to write this foreword long before coming across Mary's kind words. Her book had truly gotten under my skin before I had read them, for reasons I'll point to herein.

Mary's parents, Walt and Milly Woodward, are best known as defenders of the Constitution—newspaper editors on Bainbridge Island, due west of Seattle, who, after Pearl Harbor, stood against the internment of Japanese Americans when nearly everywhere else there was assent. The Woodwards are civil rights heroes, journalists lauded by other journalists, champions of freedom, and servants of

While at times it may have seemed to Walt and Milly Woodward, above, that reporting on the exclusion and the war as well as typical small community newspaper fare took up all their time, they did occasionally find time to escape. One of their preferred ways to spend leisure time was in their garden. The garden was so substantial, they even had a horse to help them plow.

democracy, and, duly celebrated, commemorated, and eulogized, they've gotten all the credit they deserve while losing their humanity. Thankfully, their daughter's book now goes a long way toward resurrecting Walt and Milly as complex and nuanced human beings. Her parents look no less iconic in these pages than they did before them, but herein Milly is a rose enthusiast who fertilizes with salmon carcasses, and Walt is a householder clutching a potted plant in his right hand and leaning on a baby stroller with his left. Herein Walt dominates the dinner conversation, while Milly, an honors grad at the University of Washington, nods, smiles, and washes the dishes. Walt hams for a "manning the phones" portrait; Milly warbles in the Bainbridge Island Choristers. Walt and Milly, eating breakfast amid clutter, or engaged in a puckered, septuagenarian kiss, or, with their salad days behind them, sitting like teenage lovers on the bow of their boat while anchored in the San Juan Islands.

A book like this one is in peril of a nostalgia that ultimately estranges us from history. No daughter, after all, is objective about her parents, or entirely free of a psychological burden regarding the family past that surely must weigh on her writing. An intermingling of pride, mourning, love, and gilded memory is bound to inform it, and the texture and complexity of personal feelings is bound to inhere. Then there is posterity to keep in mind, and the politics still at work among the living, and the resonance of parents in a writer's inner life, and the many impossibly complicated questions a daughter might reserve for her shrink. In the end, all of this is just plain more interesting than a biography contracted to a relative stranger. The facts, after all, are ubiquitous via Web browsers; what we have here instead are facts illuminated, facts in layers, and facts colored by intimate recollection. You can't click the mouse for that.

We have, as well, a careful chronology, and an engaging portrait, of the World War II era on a small island in Puget Sound, during which everyone of Japanese descent was made to leave. This is not a story we can ever be done with, since it has told itself, and tells itself now, and will probably continue to tell itself for as long as there are human beings to play it out. In this regard, *In Defense of Our Neighbors* provides a useful counterpoint to books such as Michelle Malkin's *In Defense of Internment: The World War II Round-Up and What It Means for America's War on Terror* (2004) and Lillian Baker's *American and Japanese Relocation in World War II: Fact,*

Fiction, and Fallacy (1990). In a larger sense, it provides a valuable perspective during any era in which fear is at the forefront of social consciousness. The political cartoonist Walt Kelly wrote during the McCarthy era that "we shall meet the enemy, and not only may he be ours, he may be us," which remains true in our own time. Another way of putting this is that blindness about ourselves never does anyone much good. In this conceit, Mary Woodward's book is a mirror.

It's also a book of photographs, which of course are no more objective than prose: if the pen is mightier than the sword, then the camera is, maybe, mightier than the bludgeon. Still, pondering the photos in these pages you can't help but learn something in the interstices of your subjective response. The faces, eyes, gestures, and expressions; the black-and-white landscapes; the group shots of children; and the charmingly retro, vaguely kitschy, color photos circa 1960 to 1980 are so variously moving, telling, and winning as to provoke repeat consideration. I was particularly taken with the photos of the Woodwards, not only because Walt and Milly were photogenic, but because their sensibilities, and sensitivities, were always so apparent when a camera was present. Good humor, brio, elan, zest for living, the comic impulse, ease in one's skin—do they make people like this anymore? What happened to that universe? It's mostly gone, which is what makes Walt and Milly already mythic, and both the photographs and the prose herein so pregnant with feeling.

A final thought: Some time ago, Mary Woodward and I sat down to talk about this book, and I was struck by one thing in particular afterward—that Mary, in many ways, is yet one more legacy of her parents, whom I'd met in the early 1980s. At that point, Milly was suffering from Parkinson's disease, and was a shadow of herself, a little canted in a wheelchair, and yet it was impossible not to note her command, even her grace, in such condition. As for Walt, I remember giving him the manuscript of my novel *Snow Falling on Cedars* in one of its early iterations, and waiting indefinitely for a response, and eventually knocking on his door to get it, and finding Walt, by then a widower, more than vaguely irate about something not clear to me that was probably legitimate, and coming away impressed by this blunt, irascible, sharp curmudgeon. In short, these were two people who believed in themselves without any narcissism, and this, I suppose, is what I saw in Mary when we sat down to discuss the book in your hands. "There is no death, only a change of worlds," Chief Seattle is reported to have said. For Mary, working up a book about her parents, this was true in more than one way, and we, her readers, are the beneficiaries of that.

David Guterson
Bainbridge Island, Washington
March 25, 2008

From 1941 to 1963, Milly and Walt Woodward were coeditors and copublishers of the Bainbridge Review, "the only newspaper in the world," as they put it, "that cares about Bainbridge Island." For more than twenty years, reporting the Island's news was the Woodwards' passion. During World War II, they used the paper to speak out against the exclusion of their Japanese American friends and neighbors.

At our home in Bainbridge Island's Wing Point neighborhood in the 1950s, my parents had an evening ritual. My mother, Milly, would be in the kitchen preparing dinner, and I would often join her. I liked that time alone with her. I don't remember much of what we talked about, just that it was good to share the time with her as I perched on the high, yellow kitchen chair.

Then my father, Walt, would come home and suddenly the tempo would change, and dinner preparations would kick into high gear. My father's job was to make the salad. He would make a production of oiling the bowl and combining the dressing just so. Salad finished, he would get out a whole new set of utensils and combine gin and vermouth—again just so—for what he called their "preprandial libation." That's

when he got the high, yellow kitchen chair. My parents would talk about their day—or, usually, Daddy would talk and Mother would nod, and smile, and murmur "uh-huh" periodically. To be fair, Daddy's stories were always interesting, but we heard a whole lot more of his stories than Mother's.

After we kids set the table, and the casserole was heated through, and serving dishes were brought in, the five of us would gather around our big oak dining table. Once each of us three daughters had been prodded to share something of our day with the family, we were allowed to get to the fun part of dinner, which was seeing who could stare at the other longer without laughing and where we might hide the vitamin pills.

As long as we didn't get too rambunctious, this was tolerated, and our parents would converse with each other, often about local issues. These conversations ranged over a wide array of topics: nature, sports, humor, music, boating, and especially, since they owned the local newspaper, the *Bainbridge Review*, current events. Again my father tended to dominate the conversation, perhaps rehearsing next week's editorial, but Mother held her own, and when a friendly dispute prompted retrieval of the dictionary or a volume of the *Encyclopedia Britannica* from the living room, it was she who was more frequently proven correct.

We learned a lot at that family dining table while surreptitiously kicking each other under it. One of the things we learned about was the World War II exile of some of our friends' parents from Bainbridge Island.

The "relocation" was something I always knew about, and I thought everyone else on Bainbridge Island knew about it, too. After all, it had affected so many Islanders, especially the Japanese immigrants, or *Issei*, and their families who were forced to leave their homes a few months after Pearl Harbor. It didn't occur to me to question why we never talked about it in history class or why it wasn't mentioned in the history books.

In college, I did some research on how the West Coast media reacted to the forced exile of the Japanese Americans during the war. Seeing the overt racism there, I began to appreciate my parents' unusual stand at the *Review*, which was to champion the civil rights of Japanese Americans and immigrants. However, it wasn't until two very different incidents shortly after graduation in 1968 that I realized how little I understood of the personal tragedy of the exclusion.

My friend Carole and I were riding the ferry, and she was upset because her parents, *Nisei*, or second-generation Japanese Americans, had just told her they had been forced to leave their homes during the war. After a lecture at the University of Washington about the exclusion, she had asked her parents about their experiences and learned what countless other *Sansei*—third-generation Japanese—were learning: that their parents, because the pain and the shame were so great, had not been able to muster the strength to tell their children about the injustices they suffered during World War II.

Six months later, I was teaching history to a large class of seventh graders in an overcrowded classroom in Bremerton, a nearby navy town. In the unit on World War II, I told the children about what had happened to West Coast *Nikkei*, or people of Japanese descent. They were appalled. The next day, three students returned to tell me their parents had said, "Our government never would have done that. It didn't happen." There was nothing in the textbook to prove otherwise.

Those two experiences made it clear to me that something needed to change in the way we dealt with this episode in our history. The exclusion of the Nikkei—most of whom were American citizens born in this country—from their homes needed to become part of our collective memory.

In 1988, the nation acknowledged its error and offered a formal apology to those forced into "relocation" camps in 1942. (Today the euphemisms of the 1940s are seldom used in reference to the exclusion of the Japanese Americans during World War II.

The only thing that competed with Bainbridge Island and the Review *for importance in the Woodwards' lives was family. Milly, seen opposite with grandchildren (from left to right) Laurie, John, and Daniel on a beach in the San Juan islands, was a devoted mother and grandparent. Walt, above teaching grandson Brodie to steer his boat* Big Toot II *in 1979, loved sharing his passion for boating.*

A more appropriate term—concentration camp—was used by President Roosevelt and others during the war and will be used throughout this book as it is preferred by many of today's scholars.) That public action opened the gates to painful discussions in communities all along the West Coast, from Los Angeles to our suburban island. Until then, the experience had carried a burden of guilt and disgrace for those exiled which, although unwarranted, was very real. When the exclusion was finally acknowledged, Japanese Americans began to tell their stories. In many communities, the stories are sad ones of displacement, property loss, and permanent relocation. On Bainbridge, the history included these incidents as well as stories of the many who were welcomed as they returned to their prewar homes.

Nearly sixty-five years after the exclusion, as I prepared to write this book, I joined in the annual pilgrimage to the Minidoka National Monument, created at the site of a concentration camp in Idaho. Standing behind a

Whether it was boating among the many islands and inlets of Puget Sound, opposite, or celebrating their fortieth wedding anniversary in Victoria, British Columbia, as seen here, Walt and Milly enjoyed spending time together. Throughout their marriage, while publishing the Review, raising their three daughters, and spending much of their retirement out on the water, the couple was seldom apart for long.

partially restored barrack and staring at the rough, tar-papered structure, I quietly wept. I tried to imagine what it must have been like for my friends and their parents: families of five, six, or more, living for three years in a twenty-by-twenty-foot room, with only a single bare bulb for light, separated from three other families by thin walls too short to reach the ceiling. Exiled from home and imprisoned behind barbed wire because of their heritage and appearance. Denied the most basic rights guaranteed in the Constitution.

Many Island friendships have, over the years, gently enhanced my understanding of this momentous event. I will always be grateful to those friends. I am also thankful for my experience at Minidoka, which brought me new friends and further expanded my understanding of just what it was that the exiled went through. We are all indebted to the generosity of those who found the courage to share their experiences. Now, in our Island community and across the nation, we don't pretend the exclusion never happened. In our discussions and sharing of history, we can learn from those experiences, and—it is to be hoped—with the knowledge and understanding we gain, prevent something like this from happening again in our country.

The former exiles are my heroes for enduring those difficult times with grace and dignity. I am only now beginning to fully grasp the enormity of their situation. With that appreciation comes an increased respect for my parents who, as a young couple with an infant, bought a newspaper and vowed to "always strive to speak the truth, unafraid." Their idealism and their faith in our democracy spurred them to speak out against the incarceration and stand up for the civil rights of their neighbors.

While fear and old prejudices swept the country during the chaos of early 1942, my parents were making sure these Islanders, whose removal they so eloquently opposed, remained an important and active part of the community, even if they were hundreds of miles away. By doing so, my parents were already paving the way for the Nikkei's eventual return. Like those they defended, my parents are also my heroes. I am honored to tell their story.

Bainbridge Island's logging and shipping industries brought immigrants from across the globe, creating a community in which people of different backgrounds and cultures could live as neighbors. This was especially evident in school pictures, such as this 1935 Lincoln Elementary School portrait. This relatively harmonious integration would be interrupted after the United States entered into World War II.

THE CALM BEFORE THE STORM

On October 17, 1941, Milly and Walt Woodward gave their hearts to a small-town weekly newspaper with a circulation of about one thousand, serving a quiet, rural island in the Puget Sound. The paper, the *Bainbridge Review*, had been my parents' venture for more than a year. With high hopes, they bought the *Review* in July 1940 with two good friends, Lawrence and Claire Peters, a lawyer and a schoolteacher, but they had not been able to find much time to work on it or to infuse it with their spirit. My father, Walt, had been living two lives, working full time as a court reporter for the *Seattle Times*, and taking the evening ferry to Bainbridge Island, rolling up his sleeves at the *Review* to write editorials, set type, and tinker with the temperamental machinery of their ancient flatbed press. My mother, Milly, had a double life of her own: while caring for my sister Carolyn, who was barely a toddler at the time, she shared nearly all the duties at the paper with Walt, from writing and editing to ordering newsprint to paying the bills. After a year and a half as overworked publishers, neither felt like they were living their dream.

So they changed course. In September 1941, they bought their partners' share of the paper, and in October, Walt walked away from the *Seattle Times* after six years of reporting, joining Milly full time as copublisher and coeditor of the *Bainbridge Review*. Operating from a modest, wood-framed structure near Lynwood Center, on the Island's south shore, they set up living quarters on one side of the building and published the *Review* from the other. They became devoted, jack-of-all-trades journalists. On any given day, Walt would later explain, he and Milly might each wear the hats of "newspaper owners, publishers, editors, reporters, advertising salesmen, business managers, typesetters, stereotypers, printers, pressmen, mailers, and janitors." In their early thirties they were the sole owners of a newspaper, and they were together at the helm. "Excited and serious" about the challenge, they began to make the paper their own.

For Milly and Walt, their newfound enthusiasm was front-page news. It was customary in the mid-twentieth century for small-town newspaper editors to address their readers, directly and in a personal manner, about themselves, the paper, the community, and the issues of the day, and my parents used the device to great effect. In the months ahead, when war would break out in the Pacific and widespread fear about "enemy aliens" would undermine the civil rights of many Americans, my parents would use the *Review* to speak out vigorously in defense of democratic principles and community values. After Pearl Harbor, the *Review* would stand virtually alone among newspapers in its opposition to the exclusion and incarceration of Japanese Americans—an issue of enormous significance throughout the nation and certainly on tiny Bainbridge Island, where nearly three hundred Japanese Americans resided in the early 1940s. Just as important, the *Review* would also become a healing force, a spacious public square where weekly accounts of life by Bainbridge Island Japanese Americans in the camps—covering the extremes of desert weather and strange food, as well as births, deaths, and baseball scores—could be read alongside harvest reports, tide charts, shipbuilding news, and letters to the editor. By bridging the crowded, dusty California and Idaho camps with rural, maritime Bainbridge Island, the *Review* would keep alive the community's connection with its separated residents throughout the war.

MILLY LOVES WALTIE TSK LTSK TSK —

From his days at the Seattle Times, *Walt, shown opposite working on the* Review's *linotype, was a seasoned journalist. Once he and Milly purchased the* Review, *they had to take on all the tasks of running a newspaper, from writing and editing articles to selling advertising and running the presses. Above: One of the first lines of type cast on their linotype.*

But when they committed themselves to the paper in the autumn of 1941, my parents simply wanted to let the Bainbridge Island community know that they were in it for the long haul. Their declaration of commitment, an upbeat editorial titled "We Choose the Review," shared the front page with stories on changing ferry schedules, the opening of deer hunting season, and the hoped-for improvement of the Island's notoriously rugged dirt roads.

We're together now in this business of publishing The Review. We've taken a deep breath, drawn up our own Declaration of Independence, cut all business connections we had with Seattle, and thrown our permanent lot with Bainbridge Island.

Given the growing preponderance of articles about the threat of war in nearly every newspaper, the October 17 *Review* was refreshingly light. But what this first paper lacked in hard-hitting stories, my parents more than made up for in commitment:

So . . . our pledge to you is this: A Review which will be crammed to the column rules with news while it is still news; a Review which will be bright, sparkling and thought provoking in its features, photographs and columns; lastly—and perhaps most important—a Review which will always strive to speak the truth, unafraid, whether it be on a national issue or something purely local.

In an accompanying news article, Walt summed up my parents' new sense of commitment: "We seek the Island's friendship and support, for we intend to make The Review our life's work."

The island with which Walt and Milly sought fellowship was both a world of its own and a place that had always been shaped by forces beyond its shores, from the mammoth glaciers that carved the island's terrain to the enterprising nineteenth-century businessmen who transformed a landscape of ancient forests and deep, pristine harbors into an industrial powerhouse. In 1941, in fact, Bainbridge Island was only a few decades removed from its early glory years, when the Port Blakely Mill Company and the Hall Brothers Shipbuilding Firm commanded the world's attention.

An Island Oasis for Immigrants

Japanese, Italians, Swedes, Basques, Filipinos, Finns, and immigrants from around the globe came to Bainbridge Island during the booming years of the Port Blakely Mill, which began in the 1870s. They worked together by day and returned to separate worlds at night. Those "worlds" consisted of a New Sweden, a so-called Dagotown, and a Yama, the Japanese settlement. There were also communities of Austrian fishermen at Eagle Harbor and Wing Point, a Hawaiian village, native Suquamish on the hillsides surrounding Port Blakely, and Chinese cooks and waiters near their jobs at the hotel.

The differences that separated Port Blakely's ethnic communities were formidable, but the shared experience of making a life on Bainbridge Island brought people together. Differences in language and race seemed minuscule compared to the bounty that could be reaped from the Island through shared effort. Isami "Sam" Nakao, who grew up in Yama, remembered how "the Peterson farm at Fort Ward supplied the cream for Takayoshi's ice cream parlor," and how "the Peterson family and people from all over came here to eat ice cream." Young boys and girls from various communities fished off the docks for perch and cod using hand lines and homemade hooks. The Loverich family, sailors and shipbuilders from the Adriatic Sea, hired a Japanese captain, Katsu Hamachi, to skipper one of their fishing boats. It was a progressive choice for a time not far removed from the days of the 1889 U.S. Census, when Japanese workers at the Port Blakely mill were still being listed as Jap 1, Jap 2, and Jap 3.

Bainbridge Island before World War II was dotted with many small neighborhoods, each with its own steamship landing, post office, grocery, and gathering place. Isolated overland by the few heavily rutted roads, the neighborhoods were easily accessible by the "Mosquito Fleet" steamers, whose nickname aptly described the boats as they darted about, touching at some of the Island's numerous docks before crossing Puget Sound to tie up at the "big city" of Seattle. Islanders were so in tune with their steamboats, they knew which captain was at the helm by the timbre of its whistle as it docked.

As children of neighboring communities entered the Island's several elementary and secondary schools, a unifying element was created. Relationships between children of all backgrounds were especially rich. Even during the days of Dagotown and New Sweden, remembered Chiye Shigemura Umezuka, "the children from all the settlements went everywhere, free of the language barriers faced by their parents, and mixed together in the schools."

In 1928, the school district consolidated the two hundred older students into Bainbridge High School, whose grounds were enhanced in 1935 by five Japanese cherry trees, a gift of the six Japanese American graduates of 1934 and their Issei parents. The trees, relocated to make way for construction at the high school in 2007, now grace the campus of Sonoji Sakai Intermediate School, named in honor of one of those Issei.

At Bainbridge High School, children and grandchildren of millworkers, lumberjacks, farmers, maids, wealthy landowners, and service providers came together as classmates and developed friendships that cut across social and economic lines.

The 1938 Bainbridge High School yearbook shows a student council composed of Sally Miller, Ebo Okazaki, Takashi Sakuma, and Sylvia Svornich. The year's theatrical productions included *The Wedding* and *The Kakemono of Nagoshigii*, the latter of which was performed in traditional Japanese dress. The clubs and sports teams displayed similar diversity, launching cross-cultural friendships that endured beyond high school years. Gerald "Jerry" Nakata, who graduated from Bainbridge High in 1941, said he and his school buddies, Hal Champeness and Earl Hanson, remained "the closest of friends" throughout their lives. They met in grade school, became pals fishing and playing baseball, and graduated together in June. "Six months later," Nakata said, "Pearl Harbor happened. And then we got closer."

Over the years, casual associations between adults also grew into family friendships and a relatively harmonious Island culture. The Loverichs from southern Europe and the Nakatas, one of the original Yama families, became close and would ultimately go into business together, opening the Town & Country Market after the war. Gary Loverich, the elder Loverich's grandson, surmises that the two patriarchs—the big-boned and jovial Loverich and the modest and reserved Nakata—met on an Island beach while digging clams.

When the saw mill closed in the early 1920s, the various immigrant settlements dispersed, further integrating the Island. The Japanese, for example, became strawberry farmers, greenhouse operators, grocers, and barbers. Settling where they found land or opportunity, their neighbors were as likely to be Swedish or Irish as Japanese. On the strawberry farms, the pickers were often First Nation natives from Canada and immigrants from the Philippines. Many Filipino men married Coast Salish women—in 1942 alone there were twelve such weddings—thereby further enriching the Island with Indopino families.

Located in the northwest corner of the U.S., near the westernmost point of the contiguous states, Bainbridge Island was undeveloped country and a land of opportunity. It was an oasis for immigrants—although one they had to work very hard to create for themselves. In a sense, the frontier, homesteading mind-set that populated the entire country was played out in microcosm on this hilly, wooded island.

In an era when ethnic groups typically kept to themselves, on Bainbridge Island the shared quest for prosperity prompted members of various immigrant groups to work together. Katsu Hamachi, shown far left with two unidentified men, captained a fishing boat for Tom Loverich, a Croatian immigrant.

The lumber mill, considered the largest in the world in the late nineteenth century, produced up to 120 million board feet of lumber a year, or roughly fifty miles of foot-wide planks every day. Issac, Winslow, and Henry Knox Hall, the West Coast's most celebrated shipwrights, built sailing ships and steamers with planks cut at the Port Blakely mill—the mill and the yard were connected by rail—and designed schooners to carry Port Blakely lumber to markets along the Pacific Coast and in Hawaii. Meanwhile, ships from all over the world, from ports in Sweden, Spain, Finland, Peru, South Africa, and Australia, crowded the harbor, waiting in what one observer called a "great forest of masts" for a coveted load of gargantuan Douglas fir beams.

As the mill grew, so did the mill town. Jobs were plentiful, and workers came from as many places as there were boats in the harbor, often jumping ship to join logging crews or load lumber schooners for one dollar a day or, if that went bad, to fish and farm. Kamekichi Shibayama, who eventually became a wealthy Island entrepreneur, was one such man. Another immigrant, Swedish farmer Nils Elofson, rowed buckets of milk out to thirsty sailors. Torazo Nakao, a Japanese millworker dubbed "Slab Harry," worked a second job overseeing the provision of castaway slabs of lumber to steamships, which burned them for fuel. A seventy-five-room hotel accommodated a widening stream of tourists and businesspeople. By 1895, a visiting reporter observed that Port Blakely was "one of the busiest and most thriving towns on the Pacific Coast."

The thriving town was in fact many towns. There was the company town, a boardwalk avenue of neat workers' cottages and administrators' homes that ran along the busy waterfront between the mill and the shipyard, and then there were the outlying neighborhoods, each hosting one of the many ethnic groups who had made Bainbridge Island home.

Bainbridge did not just attract immigrants and industrialists, though. As Seattle began to grow in the late nineteenth century, some of its inhabitants longed to get away from the city—and a few found refuge on the pretty island nearby. Soon, the shoreline began sprouting the summer homes of Seattle's well-to-do alongside bachelors' cabins, beachcombers' shacks, and the tent platforms and cabins of middle-class families and campers.

Although Bainbridge Island was only eight miles from Seattle, it had few of the amenities of its larger, metropolitan neighbor. The quickest, most efficient way to get around was by boat rather than automobile. The scattered roads were no more than rough dirt corridors, alternating between mud and dust depending on the season, and oiled only very occasionally in summer as the county budget allowed. Among the young people the common means of land transportation was walking, since with the Depression and the sad state of the roads, the automobile was still a bit of a novelty.

As the Island developed, its mix of residents continued to be nearly as diverse as could be found in the Northwest. These residents became Walt and Milly's neighbors, the people who inspired them to make the *Review* their life's work. It must have been a decision made out of love, because the pair had no formal training in journalism. While Walt did have seven years of reporting experience—covering sports for a newspaper in Juneau, Alaska, and reporting for a radio station there in addition to his court beat for the *Seattle Times*—he had never been an editor or publisher. Milly, for her part, had diverse interests and accomplishments—University of Washington honors graduate, proficient writer and speaker of Japanese, former habitué of Seattle's bohemian Blue Moon Tavern, recreational mountaineer—but she was not a journalist. After majoring in what was then called "Oriental Studies," she became a schoolteacher, eventually devoting herself to *Review*.

In fact, they met in her classroom in Juneau. Covering a high school sporting event for the *Juneau Empire*, Walt walked into a room expecting to interview the coach of the local team. Instead, he

Loggers like Zenhichi Harui (left) and Kaichi Seko (second from the right) along with two unidentified men, above, cut the trees for processing in the Port Blakely mill, which in turn produced the raw materials for the Hall Brothers shipyard, opposite. After the mill shut down in the 1920s, strawberry farming took over as a major Island industry. Workers kept track of the berries they picked with punch cards, below.

The bustling city of Seattle was visible across Puget Sound, yet Islanders found themselves secluded from the rest of the world—and even other parts of the Island. Rutted roads made overland travel on the Island difficult, and regular ferry service between Bainbridge and Seattle wasn't established until 1923, so Islanders relied on Mosquito Fleet steamers like the Hyak through the early 1930s.

The Island Issei's Rich Heritage

One hundred years ago, Bainbridge Island's Port Blakely was the bustling center of Puget Sound industry. Massive cargo ships maneuvered before the mammoth, 44,000-square-foot, central building. Forges, woodshops, and freight and hay warehouses surrounded the ubiquitous boiler house, which boasted a 300-horsepower boiler that belched smoke from burning sawdust, "lighting up the sky with flames and cinders." Just a few hundred feet above that maelstrom of activity, shielded by a growth of alder and fir, was the bustling town of Yama, which housed some three hundred Japanese in about fifty homes.

The first Japanese on the Island jumped ship in Port Blakely and spent their off hours gambling and drinking in a cluster of dwellings called Nagaya (which translates as "valley"). Before long, these *wataridori* (birds of passage) moved on and were replaced by other men interested in establishing families. With the help of the traditional *baishakunin* (go-between), these bachelors arranged for picture brides. One such woman left her safe Japanese home in 1897 and sailed for fourteen days across an ocean to meet the stranger who was to be her husband. Together, Mitsue and Yasuji Suyematsu established what has become one of Bainbridge's oldest and most respected families.

With lumber donated by the mill, these immigrants and others built their homes above Nagaya. Yama (mountain) was like the hillside villages its residents had left behind. The simple, unpainted houses were crowded so closely together on the steep hillside that they appeared literally on top of each other. They were interspersed with productive truck gardens and patios dripping with wisteria and scattered with bonsai. Inside the homes, paint and wallpaper brightened the walls. A planked road followed a stream up the hill to a Buddhist temple, a Baptist mission, and the community playfield.

Like most immigrants, the children started school knowing only their parents' native language. The men learned some English through their jobs, but the women spoke Japanese almost exclusively. While many women adopted Western dress, they wore kimonos for special occasions. They served traditional Japanese meals, prepared with fresh produce from their gardens, perch from the millpond, salmon and rock cod from the harbor, clams and *nori* (dried seaweed) from the beaches, and matsutake mushrooms from the forest.

Yama had many of the amenities that make life interesting. The enterprising "General" Tamegoro Takayoshi provided several: along with grocery and laundry service, he offered an ice cream parlor that, with its piano, doubled as a dance hall; a photography studio; a watch repair shop; and a tea house. The Kono family ran the two-and-a-half-story Washington Hotel, which had ten rooms and a Western-style restaurant serving fresh bread from their bakery. The Shigemuras ran another restaurant offering freshly baked goods. There were three Japanese bathhouses, two barber shops, and a tofu shop, and mail and newspapers were delivered daily.

Yama flourished from 1890 until after World War I, when it began to wither as the mill grew less productive. After the mill closed in the early 1920s, the town was eventually demolished, and many Island Nikkei turned to farming.

By 1941, Island Japanese had become proficient in strawberry farming and were within grasp of economic stability after long decades of hard work. One such farmer, Sonoji Sakai, could not have succeeded without help from local grocer Thomas Loverich. So frequently did Sakai have to call on his friend for help that Loverich often greeted him good naturedly in his loud booming voice with, "Old Man Sakai! Not you again?" A Croatian immigrant, Loverich arrived on Bainbridge in 1903 with his wife, Christina. Like many small-town grocers, they frequently carried a farmer's account for a year or more until a successful harvest allowed him to pay off his debt.

On land where huge, first-growth forests had been felled for the lumber mills and mammoth stumps—some eight feet in diameter—remained, Island Japanese took on the difficult job of stump removal to reveal fields of sandy loam. Ultimately they cleared much of the land where today's houses stand. The children worked alongside their parents with the babies, as Masaharu "Mutt" Yamashita recalled, "out in the field in an old [empty] dynamite box." Teenagers came home from school to a snack of rice balls, explained Kazuko "Kay" Sakai Nakao in 1983, then changed clothes and "hustled out to work two or three hours." Weekends, too, found the family in the field.

The unrelenting labor took decades, but by the late 1930s many Japanese farm families were breathing a little easier and beginning to anticipate some financial stability, explained Hisako "Hisa" Hayashida Matsudaira. "Just five years before the evacuation, many families were starting to be successful and had built new houses," she said.

As the Issei became more prosperous, the farmers recruited help for the harvest from First Nation natives from British Columbia and new immigrants from the Philippines. The farmers' selling practices also changed. The Moritanis first brought berries to market in a wheelbarrow before canning became routine. By 1923, the original processing operation in the Sumiyoshis' kitchen had evolved into the Winslow Berry Growers Association's cannery. In 1940, the farmers, in association with the R. D. Bodle Company, sent two million pounds of Bainbridge Island's prized Marshall berries to market.

Fumiko Nishinaka Hayashida, a strawberry farmer who was pregnant in the spring of 1942, remembered thinking, "After all these years paying for the equipment, this crop might come out ahead." The plants, in full bloom in March, would probably be ready for harvest in April, a month or two ahead of schedule. Everything pointed to a good harvest.

After the lumber mill closed, many Island Japanese families turned to farming. Below, Ohtohiko Koura (right) on his farm with R. D. Bodle, who owned a berry canning company based in Seattle. Bottom: A crate commonly used by strawberry pickers. Opposite: A broken tea cup is one of the few relics that still remain from the Japanese town of Yama.

Milly, above (second from left), on her family's farm near Ephrata, Washington, spent summers on the Island with her parents and her siblings (from left to right) Evelyn, David, and Elmer. Milly and Walt, opposite above with daughter Carolyn Jane, moved to the Island after they married. Together, they renovated Milly's grandmother's dilapidated house, opposite below, for their growing family.

fell hard for Milly Logg, a tall, bright, attractive redhead from Bainbridge Island. Milly fell for Walt, too, charmed by the affable doctor's son with the easy laugh and wry wit. Less than a year later, they were married in Seattle.

One of five surviving children, Milly was born in a log cabin on Bainbridge Island to a mother who raised pigs and chickens, cured bacon, annually filled a root cellar, and bedded her children in a sleeping porch "up the hill," since the family home was too small. Milly scandalized her father by bobbing her hair in the 1920s and worked her way through the UW as part of the high-spirited summer staff at Paradise Inn in the Mount Rainier National Park. She was tough and smart: once, a solitary mountain walk ended as the clouds rolled in, and she sat all night in the cold rather than risk a return trek over rough terrain with limited visibility.

Both sets of Milly's grandparents had homesteaded on Bainbridge Island in the nineteenth century after years of wheat farming in eastern Washington. Her father continued in the wheat business and brought his young family to Bainbridge to escape the summer heat on the other side of the Cascade Mountains. When she and Walt married, they built their first home on family land.

Walt was the son of prominent Seattle physician Walter C. Woodward Sr., whose own father had been a conductor on the Vermont Underground Railroad, which helped slaves escape to freedom a century earlier. Walt's parents grew up in Randolph, Vermont. After becoming engaged to marry, they traversed the country in separate train trips to reach Seattle, which was still rebuilding in the early 1900s after its disastrous 1889 fire. A high school journalist, Walt became a pre-med student at the UW and seemed to be following his father into medicine. There, he was also part of the legendary Clarence "Hec" Edmundson's track team, and earned a

prized "Good job, Woody!" after a
particularly fine effort as a miler
against Oregon State.

But neither science nor sport
took hold in Walt, and he soon
realized his real passion for
communications. Inheriting his
father's dry sense of humor, Walt
was a master craftsman with
words, using them to amuse,
educate, and inspire. He loved
a good yarn. In 1935, Walt was
among the last to interview one
of his personal heroes, humorous
pundit Will Rogers, before Rogers
and Wiley Post flew to their deaths
near Point Barrow in the far
Alaskan north.

Walt commuted by ferry—and
during frequent ferry strikes, by
open boat—to his *Seattle Times* job

before turning to the *Review* full time in the fall of 1941. Milly ran the library
and taught English and sociology at Bainbridge High School. Former students
remember her as "someone you looked up to and respected," a pretty lady, her
hair in a French twist, who was always willing to take time for a student.

Walt and Milly came from different backgrounds. Milly was a self-
described bohemian while Walt had conservative parents who referred to
Franklin Delano Roosevelt disdainfully as "that man in the White House."
But once Walt and Milly were on the job together, the *Review* made true
journalists out of both of them. If Walt had a perpetually bruised toe from
kicking a finicky press he could never quite fix, he also had a nose for news
and an instinctual grasp of storytelling. In a *Review* column after Walt's death
in 2001, Wayne Jacobi, a colleague of Walt and Milly's during the 1950s,
called Walt "a newspaperman's newspaperman," an honor worth a handful
of Pulitzers. Milly didn't get such accolades in print, but the compliment
applied to her as well. She was a clear, fair-minded reporter, an engaging
columnist, and an effective editor.

Perhaps most important, my parents transcended formal training with
heart. The news mattered because it mattered to the Hansons and the Ohtakis and the
Loverichs and the Nakaos. And so the paper was indeed "crammed to the column rules" with news for their

With the Warspite editorial causing a nationwide stir and the growing threat of war testing the couple in their new roles, Walt and Milly were able to find solace in each other and their family. With his perennial good humor, Walt stayed focused on developments at the paper while Milly split her time between the paper and caring for their daughter Carolyn, opposite.

neighbors, news ranging from the rising price of milk at Island dairies to the record output at the strawberry packing plant—nearly four million pounds during the early summer of 1941. It also covered the increasing presence of the U.S. Navy, which in 1941 hired the Winslow Marine Railway and Shipbuilding Company to build four steel minesweepers, a contract the *Review* called "the largest single industrial development in the history of Bainbridge Island."

The prewar *Review* showed its mettle and strong principles as well, disregarding a navy request for voluntary censorship on reports of a damaged British warship, the *Warspite*, that was docked for repairs at the Bremerton shipyard in late summer 1941. At the time, the U.S. had not entered World War II and was officially providing no aid to combatants on either side of the conflict.

The *Warspite*'s presence was an open secret in the Northwest. Escorted by U.S. Navy tugs, the ship passed within several hundred feet of Bainbridge Island, and Walt walked down to the beach near the *Review*'s office to take pictures. Also, some of the 1,200 British sailors—in uniform with the ship's name on their caps—regularly took the Bremerton ferry to Seattle for shore leave.

Walt and Milly were obliged to report the truth. "We felt that the government was robbing the

American public of knowledge it should have of the United States' international policy," Walt explained in a 1968 informal community talk. "We heartily approved of giving aid in our navy yards to battered British men o' war, but we were convinced the American public should know about it."

The *Review*'s story, the first to disclose the presence of the warship, was not repeated by the Seattle papers, but it went out on the United Press wire and was ultimately picked up by *Time* magazine, which quoted liberally from the couples' editorials and news articles.

If the *Warspite* editorial stance had been their first test, my parents would soon face a much greater challenge. Just three months after that editorial, and a matter of weeks after Walt left the *Seattle Times*, the Japanese attack on Pearl Harbor reverberated across the Pacific. Walt and Milly Woodward's *Review*, "The Only Newspaper in the World That Cares About Bainbridge Island," was suddenly reporting to a community torn apart by war.

On the morning of March 30, 1942, soldiers removed the Island's Japanese American families from their homes and gathered them at Eagledale Dock to await transport off the Island to a final destination unknown to the community. The families huddled together at the dock were given only six days to prepare for their evacuation. They had no idea when they would be allowed to return.

2

THE FIRST
STIRRINGS OF
EXCLUSION

WAR EXTRA!

Bainbridge Island - Gem of Puget Sound

BAINBRIDGE REVIEW

BEST WEEKLY IN THE NORTHWEST

Published every Friday; entered as second-class matter, Port Blakely, Washington

BAINBRIDGE ISLAND, WASHINGTON, MONDAY, DEC. 8, 1941. VOL. XVII, NO. 31. (EXTRA)   ONE PAGE, 5 CENTS

ISLAND DEFENSE SET!

BAINBRIDGE REVIEW

Bainbridge Island, Washington
Office and plant located at Pleasant Beach
Telephone Port Blakely 80

An Independent Newspaper Published Every Week Since May, 1925
Entered as second-class matter September 4, 1925, at the Post Office at Rolling Bay, Washington, and reentered February 9, 1940, at the Post Office at Port Blakely, Washington, under the Act of March 3, 1897.

WALTER C. WOODWARD, JR. and MILDRED LOGG WOODWARD
PUBLISHERS

Member: Washington Newspaper Publishers' Association
Winner Honorable Mention, 1941 General Excellence Contest of National Editorial Association

PLAIN TALK

If there ever was a community which faced a local emergency growing out of something over which it had no control, it is Bainbridge Island this Monday morning in December, 1941.

This is no time to mince words.

There are on this Island some 300 members of 50 families whose blood ties lie with a nation which, yesterday, committed an atrocity against all that's decent.

The great American democracy is a slow-moving creature, at best. We Americans dilly-dally around, talk a lot, fool with labor strikes and in many other ways give apparent evidence that we are not as efficient as a smooth-working Nazi machine.

But you don't treat America the way Japan treated America without swift, sudden and sure action.

And in such a recoil of sentiment here is the danger of a blind, wild hysterical hatred of all persons who can trace ancestry to Japan. That some of those persons happen to be American citizens, happen to be loyal to this country and happen to have no longer a binding tie with the fatherland are factors which easily could be swept aside by mob hysteria.

So, once again, The Review points out to Island Japanese that they cannot change their names as did Germans in the last war. They must stand on the facts as they are. They are Japanese-Americans and America is at war with Japan.

Island Japanese, as never before, must prove their mettle as loyal Americans. They must realize they will be the objects of intense scrutiny. They must not resent this. They must welcome it. They must do everything in their power to ferret out those among their number—if any there be—who do not have an abiding love and loyalty for this America of ours.

To other Islanders, The Review says this: These Japanese-Americans of ours haven't bombed anybody. In the past, they have given every indication of loyalty to this nation. They have sent, along with our boys, their own sons—six of them—into the United States Army. They, in this edition, are quoted as pledging anew their loyalty.

So, of all Islanders—Japanese and otherwise—The Review would seek as calm an approach to this emergency as possible. Let us so live in this trying time that when it is all over that loyal Americans can look loyal Americans in the eye with the knowledge that, together, they kept the Stars and Stripes flying high over the land of the brave and the home of the free.

Mrs. Osgood, Friend Of Japanese, Dies

Mrs. Anna Osgood, long a friend and patron of Island Japanese, did not live to learn of Japan's hostilities against the United States.

The victim of a heart attack, she died at her Manitou home at 2 o'clock yesterday morning, just a few hours before the Island heard radio broadcasts telling of Japan's bombing of this nation's Far East defense posts.

"It is a merciful thing for her that she died before this attack by Japan occurred," said Mrs. Fred F. Weld, Manitou, long a personal friend of Mrs. Osgood. "Japanese hearts in this community will be heavy not only for what Japan has done. They also will mourn Mrs. Osgood, for she was their good friend."

Complete details on the funeral were not determined late last night, but it was learned the service will be held tomorrow from the Bonney-Watson Company, Seattle.

Mrs. Osgood and her husband, the Rev. Robert S. Osgood, who survives her, came to Bainbridge Island in 1912, when Mr. Osgood accepted a teaching position at the Moran School for Boys, Manitou, now known as the Puget Sound Naval Academy.

They literally "pioneered" the Osgood home, carving it out of a wilderness of underbrush and trees.

Almost from the beginning of her Island residence, Mrs. Osgood took a keen interest in the task of teaching first-generation Japanese the English language and the American way of living. She fostered a class where older Japanese learned a few English words and were taught to understand the American schooling their children were receiving.

Born in Iowa as Anna Adams, Mrs. Osgood met her husband in Grinnell, Ia. They had no children.

During the World War, Mr. Osgood went overseas as an Army chaplain. During his absence, Mrs. Osgood filled his place in the pulpit of the Winslow Congregational Church.

Her wide circle of friends mourned her not only as a lovely woman but as one who always was willing to do things for other people.

This Issue . . .

This edition of The Review, hurriedly prepared by a short-

Spare That Tree!

JAPANESE LEADERS HERE PLEDGE LOYALTY TO AMERICA

The Island's more than 300 residents of Japanese extraction hear yesterday's war news with the realization they must prove to the community and the nation that they are loyal Americans, their leaders told The Review last night.

Pledges of loyalty to the United States were prompt from those leaders. Here are the hastily-gathered comments of a few Island-Japanese:

H. O. Koura, Manzanita, president of the Japanese Chamber of Commerce—I am completely taken by surprise. I had heard talks of conflict between Japan and the United States, but I never realized it would reach this conclusion. Seventy years ago, through the aid of the United States, Japan was opened to the world and through this became a modernized nation. I never, therefore, expected to see Japan in conflict with the United States.

I came to this nation thirty years ago, and have been on the Island for twenty, I am the father of six children, all of whom have been educated in the public schools here. My sole purpose is to raise those children to be good members of American society.

Some Japanese families already have sent their young men into active United States military service. Therefore, speaking in behalf of the Japanese Chamber of Commerce, I am positive every Japanese family on the Island has an intense loyalty for the United States of America and stands ready to defend it.

John Nakata, Winslow, Island grocer—I was born and raised on Bainbridge Island and feel I am a 100 per cent American citizen. I know that I, and others similarly situated, feel a great loyalty to this nation. We will protect our flag. Our flag is the United States flag.

Art Koura, Island chairman of the Japanese-American Citizens' League, son of H. O. Koura—I know our league will do everything it can to help the defense of this nation. Every Japanese, first or second generation, will do everything he can to protect this nation's flag.

If there is any sign of sabotage or spies, we will be the first ones to report it to the authorities.

I think Japan is "nutty" to try this.

CHURCH BELLS HUSHED

Laurance A. Peters, local defense commissioner, late last night issued the following urgent requests to all Islanders:

LEADERS PREPARE FOR BLACKOUT!

Only a few hours after the outbreak of hostilities between Japan and the United States, Bainbridge Island late last night was prepared—temporarily, at least—for an air-raid bombing or other serious emergency.

A meeting of the local defense commission was called promptly by Laurance A. Peters, local defense commissioner, yesterday afternoon. All sub-chairmen were represented at the meeting at his Port Blakely home last night.

An air-raid blackout signal system, details of which may be found elsewhere in this edition, was established. It will rely on church bells, industrial plant whistles and automobile horns.

Defense leaders, taking the attitude that "anything can happen," warned Islanders to be on the alert to blackout electric lights upon warning.

Island watchers for the Interceptor Command went on a 24-hour basis.

Japanese community pledged loyalty to the United States.

At least one Island Japanese was arrested for questioning by the Federal Bureau of Investigation.

Guards were trebled at the Island's Naval Radio Station and at the Winslow Marine Railway and Shipbuilding Company.

The Pacific Telephone and Telegraph Company and the Puget Sound Power and Light Company indicated extra steps would be taken to guard their facilities here.

Arrangements were being made to bring summer fire-fighting equipment, stored for the winter at Port Orchard, back to the Island this week.

There were other developments, but they were closely guarded secrets.

Ensign L. I. Nadeau, representing Comdr. B. C. Purrington, U. S. N., commander of the Naval Radio Station, addressed the defense commission meeting. While most of his remarks were considered military secrets, this much was disclosed:

Military and naval intelligence units have the situation in hand and are taking proper local steps to guard against spies and sabotage; the Naval Radio Station went on a pre-arranged war plans basis immediately; Island civilians, led by their local defense commission, must do whatever they can, independent of military and naval aid, to safeguard homes and communities from or against sabotage or bombing.

The following sub-chairmen

Working throughout the night of December 7, Milly and Walt produced the only extra edition in the Review's history, opposite. In it, they informed Islanders of the local plans to keep them safe, and, most important, called for calm and reason in dealing with the local Japanese American community. Below: A Civil Defense helmet worn by air raid wardens on the Island during the war.

On the morning of December 7, 1941, the Empire of Japan's Imperial Japanese Navy conducted two waves of aerial attacks on the United States Pacific Fleet base at Pearl Harbor, Hawaii. More than 2,300 people were killed and almost 1,200 injured. Radio reports that Japan had attacked the base in Hawaii stunned Americans, and Bainbridge Islanders were no exception. Intent on getting crucial news to the community, Milly and Walt worked through the night and into the morning of December 8 putting together the one and only extra edition in the *Review*'s history—a one-page, single-sided issue that hit newsstands on Monday morning. They didn't want to make Islanders wait for vital information about air raid warnings and preparations for blackouts. After all, the next regular edition was four days away. Under a banner headline proclaiming ISLAND DEFENSE SET!, they reported on civil defense plans.

In addition to addressing the very real fears they and other Islanders had about further attacks, the couple took a look at the big picture, pondering the uncertain future facing Island Japanese. In a prominent editorial titled "Plain Talk," Milly and Walt wrote,

> If there ever was a community which faced a local emergency growing out of something over which it had no control, it is Bainbridge Island this Monday morning in December, 1941.
>
> This is no time to mince words.
>
> There are on this Island some 300 members of 50 families whose blood ties lie with a nation which, yesterday, committed an atrocity against all that is decent.
>
> [T]here is the danger of a blind, wild hysterical hatred of all persons who can trace ancestry to Japan. That some of those persons happen to be American citizens, happen to be loyal to this country and happen to have no longer a binding tie with the fatherland are factors which easily could be swept aside by mob hysteria.

From the early days of the Hall Brothers shipyard, Bainbridge Island was a shipbuilding mecca of the Pacific Northwest. During the war, the Winslow Shipyard, opposite, produced twenty steel minesweepers and a dry dock caisson for the U.S. Navy. In addition, the battleship West Virginia, *which took losses at Pearl Harbor, visited during the war. Below: A pamphlet from the company.*

They called on Island Nikkei, who could not avoid association with the enemy by simply "[changing] their names as did Germans in the last war," to "ferret out" any who were disloyal among them. The editorial closed with a call for calm in the face of war:

> To other Islanders, The Review says this: These Japanese Americans of ours haven't bombed anybody. In the past, they have given every indication of loyalty to this nation. They have sent, along with our boys, their own sons—six of them—into the United States Army. . . .
>
> Let us so live in this trying time that when it is all over loyal Americans can look loyal Americans in the eye with the knowledge that, together, they kept the Stars and Stripes flying high over the land of the brave and the home of the free.

Elsewhere in the extra were statements from prominent leaders in the Japanese community who expressed their loyalty to America. "My sole purpose is to raise [my six] children to be good members of American society," said Otohiko Koura, an Island resident for twenty years and president of the Japanese Chamber of

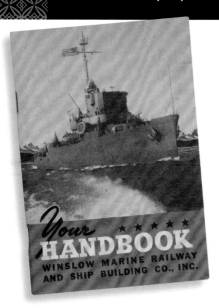

Your HANDBOOK
WINSLOW MARINE RAILWAY
AND SHIP BUILDING CO., INC.

Commerce. "I am positive every Japanese family on the Island has an intense loyalty for the United States of America and stands ready to defend it."

"I think everybody was scared. There was an explosion at the shipyard one night that had us all thinking we were being bombed," Milly remembered in a 1983 interview with Seattle producer John de Graaf for a public television documentary on the exclusion called *Visible Target*. If there were another attack, as everyone expected, people felt Bainbridge Island—which sits like a bull's-eye in the middle of Puget Sound—would likely be hit. On the Island itself were a naval intelligence station, the Winslow shipyard with its three thousand workers, and a military radio tower rising more than nine hundred feet. Surrounding the community at nearly every point on the compass were the Boeing Aircraft Company, the Seattle shipyard, the Sand Point Naval Air Station, the Bremerton Naval Shipyard, the Naval Torpedo Station at Keyport, and other strategic sites.

Special military guards appeared at these installations in short order. Anti-submarine nets stretched from the Island to span the approaches to Bremerton and Keyport. Volunteers joined recruits as anti-aircraft lookouts and batteries searched the skies where barrage balloons floated.

Church bells, the *Review* told residents, were "restricted SOLELY for air-raid warning signals." Islanders were not to drive their cars at night with the lights on. At home after dusk, they were to cover their windows so no light could escape. This rule led to a delay in the printing of the *Review's* extra, after the civil defense warden threatened to shut the paper down unless blackout curtains were applied. "We had an awful lot of windows," Walt recalled ruefully.

"[My father] used to tell us every night, 'Be careful, pull down the blinds and don't turn all the lights on. You must obey orders,'" recalled young office worker Kazuko "Kay" Sakai Nakao in a 1987 discussion.

The news from the Pacific theater heightened people's fears as Japan, in the early months of the war, overran Hong Kong, Wake Island, the Philippines, and most of the rest of Southeast Asia, while threatening both India and Australia. Americans all along the Pacific Coast felt afraid and powerless.

"It was utter, utter confusion," remarked Islander Elinor Yost in 1983. "No one knew anything really truly and rumors were flying."

West Coast Japanese knew an additional anxiety. Gerald "Jerry" Nakata, a 1941 Bainbridge High School graduate, remembered in 2001, "Oh, [we were] very, very nervous, because hey, we have the face of the enemy." They had heard the stories from World War I—how sauerkraut was renamed "liberty cabbage," how people burned transcriptions of Beethoven's works, and how, to avoid harassment, many a Schmidt anglicized his name to Smith. No such ruse was possible for them, and they were scared. They could not deny their faces and were soon to suffer the legacy of decades of vicious anti-Japanese racism.

"My immediate thought was that we . . . would be in for a very, very tough time," recalled Isami "Sam" Nakao, who at twenty-seven was one of the older Nisei. "I thought tension would be there, but when war did occur it really was a shock. I know everybody was grave, and it was a very trying time."

Island Nikkei were particularly apprehensive about what would happen to the Issei. Unable to become American citizens, they had been designated "enemy aliens" even though they had long since claimed Bainbridge as home. A concerned group of Nisei, all in their twenties, met with Walt in the *Review* office on December 8. They looked to the Woodwards for guidance despite the fact that the couple was not much older than they. The *Review*'s part-time janitor, seventeen-year-old Paul Ohtaki, heard the exchange. "They knew what an important role the newspaper had [in] the community and had come for advice and to discuss this very important and sensitive situation," he remembered in a 2001 essay in *It Was the Right Thing to Do*, his self-published compilation of *Review* articles and correspondence from that era.

Walt himself recalled that meeting in a *Seattle Times* column on December 7, 1969, twenty-eight years after the attack on Pearl Harbor:

> What, they asked, can we do to prove our loyalty to the United States of America?
>
> For one thing, I replied, you must never, never again have anything to do with a Japanese "language school;" people are suspicious of those schools, I said. At this, they laughed. The only sinister thing taught at that school, they said, was the Japanese alphabet. And most of them said they hadn't learned their lessons well.
>
> I also said they—or some of their fellow Nisei—would have to don the uniform of the United States military and stop a few bullets. They did not laugh.

Almost immediately, federal restrictions were ordered for the Issei, curtailing their right to do business and prohibiting them from traveling off the Island. These restrictions also often applied to their citizen children. When the Issei bank accounts were frozen in December 1941, the entire community was affected since most Nisei were teenagers or younger and still living at home. Island Nisei were at first prohibited from riding the ferries—their only avenue to Seattle. This was later amended to allow such travel after showing proof of country of birth. Setsuo Omoto, who was twenty-seven in 1941, recalled being stopped by an official who had been a classmate of his at Bainbridge High School. "[H]e knew full well that I was a native born on the Island, but he had to follow the regulation," Omoto said in a 1983 interview. "I was stranded in Seattle for a couple of days."

To convince the wider community of their loyalty, Island Nikkei stopped participating in activities such as judo competitions, opposite above, and the Japanese language school. They also destroyed or hid items such as the sake bottle, right, and the kimonos, opposite bottom, worn by Kay Nakao (left) and her sister Yaeko Sakai Yoshihara.

The *Review* reported in late December that "[a] truckload of radio sets, cameras, and binoculars owned by Island Japanese was taken to Port Orchard Monday in compliance with a Presidential proclamation" concerning contraband. The article quoted the deputy sheriff's praise of the Islanders' "very fine" voluntary cooperation. It also noted "some of the articles were owned by second-generation Japanese who are American citizens." The Nisei were required to surrender their property if any Issei resided with them.

Fear and uncertainty accompanied these events. The Nikkei made every effort to cooperate by reporting or turning in contraband such as dynamite, cameras, and radios. In order to demonstrate their disassociation with Japan, they burned, buried, or otherwise destroyed many precious family keepsakes. Kay Nakao recalled that her father directed the family to dispose of anything Japanese by dumping it in the outhouse. "[E]verything that we would treasure now . . . the nice things Grandmother sent us when we were children, they were just all destroyed," Nakao said.

In 1941, fearful his government would think him a spy, Henry Takayoshi, son of Yama's "General" Takayoshi, who would later go on to win several prestigious photography awards, destroyed four or five albums of his work, as well as valuable glass plate negatives that included irreplaceable photos taken aboard a four-masted sailing vessel en route to the Yukon. All were burned in the firebox of the family's outdoor *furo* (Japanese bath). What he didn't destroy "the FBI hauled off," Takayoshi recalled in a 1988 oral history conducted by the Bainbridge Island Japanese American Community (BIJAC) in preparation for a photo exhibit, part of the community's ongoing history project.

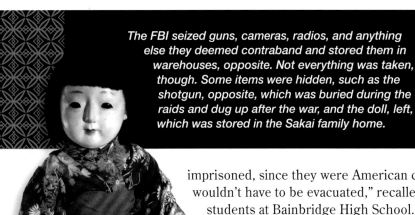

The FBI seized guns, cameras, radios, and anything else they deemed contraband and stored them in warehouses, opposite. Not everything was taken, though. Some items were hidden, such as the shotgun, opposite, which was buried during the raids and dug up after the war, and the doll, left, which was stored in the Sakai family home.

After Pearl Harbor, many Bainbridge Nikkei assumed the Issei would face internment. Long recognized internationally, internment is the legal detention of enemy aliens in wartime with mandated conditions outlined in the Geneva Conventions. But no one expected the Issei's children would be imprisoned, since they were American citizens. "For a while, we thought maybe we wouldn't have to be evacuated," recalled Noboru "Nob" Koura, one of Milly's former students at Bainbridge High School. "We thought that the Issei might be taken, but not the citizens."

In early February, the *Review* reported "more than thirty federal, state and county peace officers in a surprise one-day search of Island Japanese homes" fanned out along the Island's dusty roads. The Federal Bureau of Investigation agents, assisted by Washington State and Kitsap County law enforcement, raided all forty homes in one day. Thirty-four Islanders were arrested and taken away with little explanation. Of these, fifteen Island Issei "whose names were not revealed immediately, were turned over to agents of the Immigration and Naturalization Service and were jailed in Seattle." Some, including Hayano Moritani, the widowed mother of three children, were soon released. Eleven men were not. Most of them were taken to a Department of Justice internment camp at Fort Missoula, Montana. Some were sent to facilities in other states. "They were arresting anybody who was a teacher or leader in the community," said Paul Ohtaki.

The arrests were made as FBI agents—who arrived in "all these black cars"—confiscated rifles, radios, and dynamite, items commonly found in farmers' homes, but now labeled contraband. The rifles were used in hunting, both as sport and to supplement the larder. The surplus WWI dynamite used by farmers in clearing land had come with government approval and Kitsap County Agricultural Agent classes on its proper use. Now its possession was considered suspicious. The FBI thoroughly searched the Sakai home, as Kay Nakao's teenaged sister, Nobuko "Nobi" Sakai Omoto, watched. "We were very thankful that they did not find anything," Omoto recalled in a 1983 interview. Yet the FBI took her father. "It just hit me that he [would be] behind bars," she said. "It was a terrible shock, and all I could do was cry. I remember him trying to be cheerful and telling us to be brave and that he would be fine."

The pain of the arrests touched young and old. Hisako "Hisa" Hayashida Matsudaira, who was six at the time, remembered in 1983 that her Auntie Fumiko took the younger children into a back room so they wouldn't see how upset everyone was. Young Hisa, however, sensed it anyway: "That was the first time I saw my mother cry."

The action left Island Japanese bewildered. Families of the arrested men did not know where the Issei were, how long they would be gone, or if they would ever be seen again. Since most of the leaders of the Nikkei community were taken, this left the responsibility to the young and inexperienced Nisei, most barely out of high school and accustomed to looking to their fathers for guidance. "Most of our Issei parents were not capable of understanding all the new laws that were handed down, and not able to carry out the

In 1942, barrage balloons over the Keyport Submarine Base punctuated the calm skies behind Ann McDougall and Becky Bovick as they spent a quiet afternoon at Battle Point. With the Winslow Shipyard, two nearby naval bases, and a host of other military targets dotting the Puget Sound, Islanders were filled with a sense of impending danger throughout the war despite the tranquil surroundings.

orders that were coming from the government," explained Sam Nakao. In a time rife with anxiety and stress, these young people faced the frequently changing directives from the government with grace and courage, helping their parents—many of whom spoke little English—cope with the increasing tensions.

Not all of the Nikkei's worries came from off the Island. Jerry Nakata recalled how his seven-year-old nephew, Donald, discovered a note wedged among the canned vegetables in his parents' grocery soon after Pearl Harbor. It read, "Don't shop here. This is a Jap store."

Despite such tensions, arrests, and terse orders, as the *Review* reported, "Agents denied widespread reports that the sudden move was the beginning of a forced evacuation of Island Japanese. . . . A spokesman said, 'We do not know anything about any "evacuation" except that what we did here today was not connected with any such move.'"

Milly and Walt, however, were aware of intensifying demands by certain nationally prominent politicians and commentators for the removal and incarceration of all Japanese from the West Coast. On February 5, 1942, the day following the warrantless FBI raids on Island Japanese homes, Walt and Milly heatedly wrote another editorial, this one under the heading "More Plain Talk."

> The time has come to bear out the truth of our words, written two months ago in an extra edition of The Review. We spoke of . . . "danger of a blind, wild, hysterical hatred of all persons who can trace ancestry to Japan."

> Up and down the Pacific Coast, in the newspapers, and in the halls of Congress are words of hatred now for all Japanese, whether they be citizens of America. These words reached a shrieking crescendo when Henry McLemore, with all the intelligence of a blind pig, wrote in the Seattle Times: "Personally I hate the Japanese. And that goes for all of them."

> That may be patriotism of a hysterical degree; but it certainly isn't the kind of patriotism that will win this war. Let us think, for a moment, what would happen if the government should adopt Mr. McLemore's fervid plea for the "immediate removal of every Japanese on the West Coast to a point deep in the interior. I don't mean a nice part of the interior, either."

After noting the economic confusion that would likely result from the loss of farm production, the coeditors considered the personal devastation inherent in such an incarceration:

> But what of . . . the wreckage that it would bring to lives of thousands and thousands of loyal American citizens who can't avoid ancestry in Japan? For who—besides those so blind as Mr. McLemore—can say that the big majority of our American Japanese citizens are not loyal to the land of their birth—the United States? Their record bespeaks nothing but loyalty. Their sons are in our Army; they are heavy contributors to the Red Cross and the defense bond drive. Even in Hawaii, was there any record of any Japanese-American citizen being other than intensely loyal?

While Walt, opposite, had faith in his fellow citizens, he also knew that the anti-Japanese American rhetoric peppering the nation's newspapers would sway many. Above: Zenhichi Harui (right), owner of Bainbridge Gardens, was able to move his family to Moses Lake, Washington, before the FBI arrests. His business partner and brother, Zenmatsu Seko (left), was one of thirty-four Islanders arrested in the raids.

Like most Americans, Walt and Milly were patriotic supporters of the war effort and trusted their government. They were confident it would follow the principles guaranteed in the Bill of Rights. Today, their faith in their political leaders' good intentions may seem naïve to some, but WWII America was red, white, and blue to the core. Their concluding words reflect this and also illustrate Walt's observation in 1998 that "it kind of grew on us" that the civil rights of Islanders were at risk. In the first days of the war they dismissed McLemore and his diatribes without rejecting the possibility that the U.S. government—for wholly honorable reasons—could take just the action McLemore called for.

> The Review argues only with Mr. McLemore and his ilk. It will not dispute the federal government if it, in its considered wisdom, calls for the removal from the Coast of all Japanese. Such order—which we hope will not come—will be based on military necessities and not on hatred.

ARMY ORDERS BAINBRIDGE ISLAND CLEARED OF JAPS

Within two weeks of that editorial, on February 19, 1942, President Franklin D. Roosevelt signed Executive Order 9066 calling for the creation of areas from which "any or all persons may be excluded" by the military. His action was unanimously authorized by Congress as a military necessity, although Ohio Senator Robert A. Taft in a Senate debate called it the "sloppiest criminal law I have ever read or seen anywhere." Once assured it would apply only to Japanese, though, Taft voted in favor of the authorization.

On March 2, FDR's designated commander, Lieutenant General J. L. DeWitt, issued Public Proclamation No. 1, which defined the western portions of Washington, Oregon, the entire state of California, and parts of Arizona as areas "with respect to which, the right of any persons to enter, remain in, or leave shall be subject to whatever restriction" he might impose.

The mechanics for the forced removal of American citizens from the West Coast were now in place.

FDR seemed to include all enemy aliens, including Germans and Italians, when he authorized the Secretary of War to establish exclusion zones. Milly and Walt took him at his word. Firmly clutching their love of country, in a February 26, 1942, editorial, they applauded the decree as "a welcome answer, The Review feels, to the bigots who have shouted for the evacuation of Japanese only." The editorial reasoned:

> The President didn't aim his order at Japanese or at . . . American-Japanese citizens. . . . He was not moved by an unreasoning passion in his desire to protect military establishments when he directed the Army to move any persons—Japanese, Germans, Italians, and American citizens whether white, yellow, or black—believed to be dangerous to the safety of any military post.

> The Review hopes that the order will not mean the removal of American-Japanese citizens, for it still believes they have the right of every citizen to be held innocent and loyal until proven guilty.

> But whatever the President's order may mean for the Island's residents, The Review is glad that it will strike all fairly without bigotry and without malice.

Such was not to be the case, however. Roosevelt's order gave the army unprecedented control over civilians, and it was soon apparent that DeWitt intended to remove only the Nikkei as a group from their West Coast homes. Although some German and Italian aliens were interned, there was no wholesale incarceration of American citizens of German or Italian extraction. On the March 5, 1942, editorial page, the couple expressed their sorrow.

Because of a cruel war in which they have no part nor parcel, there are many heartsick people on this Island today. Many are sad because of the dark news that, daily, is shadowing hopes for their nation's victory. Some weep for loved ones lost in battle.

Still more are heavy hearted because they have been told that they must prepare to move from this Island—move inland to places they have never seen and amidst people who will not welcome them.

For this latter group, The Review has done what little it could do to keep them here, for The Review trusts them and believes they are good residents of this nation. Others, in the majority, have ruled otherwise. The Review—and those who think as it does—have lost.

When it was announced that everyone—including Nisei—must go, obedience and patriotism left the young Japanese Americans no choice. "We were taught to respect authority," recalled Nob Koura in 1988. "I thought that doing what they said was the best way to help our country."

DeWitt's Proclamation No. 1 made it clear that all persons of Japanese descent would eventually be removed from the westernmost parts of the Western Defense Command, the army command that encompassed Arizona, California, Idaho, Montana, Nevada, Oregon, Utah, and Washington. Initially, the government encouraged "voluntary relocation" to the east. Ichiro Nagatani, Nisei president of the local Japanese American Citizens' League, and three other Islanders traveled to Moses Lake, a small town east of the Cascade Mountains, beyond the boundary of the exclusion zone. "We found the farmers and landowners very cooperative," Nagatani wrote in 1981 to a government commission investigating the wartime exclusion, "and with consultation between our group and theirs, we were able to get a commitment from them for a farm for every family from Bainbridge Island." Despite knowing they still would be exiled from their homes, Island Nikkei were happy that they could remain together in relative freedom.

When newspapers reported on DeWitt's signing of Public Proclamation No. 1, right, ordering the removal of all Nikkei regardless of their status as citizens, the fears of the Islanders were realized. Shortly after the proclamation was signed, regional papers, opposite, announced that the army would start the removal process on Bainbridge Island.

Their hopes were soon dashed as governors of states immediately east of the exclusion zone made it clear that the exiles were not welcome. Within three weeks of its inception, DeWitt halted "voluntary migration" altogether. The sudden revocation occurred in the midst of most Islanders' negotiations. Only the Seko, Harui, and Shibayama families had been able to finalize arrangements in time to make the move to Moses Lake.

On March 24, just three weeks after Public Proclamation No. 1 was issued, soldiers marched off the ferry from Seattle to post Civilian Exclusion Order No. 1. They were met by a large group of Island Nikkei. Walt would later recall, "You could say to yourself, 'Boy, there's where we have a war.'" But the soldiers were met with no hostility. Instead, the Island Nisei politely approached

Ouster Signed by DeWitt

Owen Valley Center for Any Who Do Not Leave Voluntarily, Officials Say

U. S. army's first compulsory action to exclude enemy aliens from northwest military areas, forcible evacuation of all Japanese, aliens and natives alike, from Bainbridge Island was on order Monday. Aliens have a week to comply.

The action of the army followed a report the navy had requested the action, recounted in The Seattle Star several days ago. The navy's request was said to have been based on the facts the island overlooks the navy yard and important channels, and has upon it several naval installations of importance.

The Bainbridge Island Japanese evacuation order is signed by Lieut. Gen. John L. DeWitt, commanding general of the western defense command and the Fourth army. Evacuations under way elsewhere on the coast were still on a voluntary basis.

During this week the Bainbridge Japanese, too, can leave voluntarily, for places they choose, provided such places are approved by the army.

Notices are to go up on the Island Tuesday, ordering all Japanese to report to a new evacuation control center set up near the ferry landing. Each Japanese will be assigned a number.

All Japanese left on the island by March 30 will be taken into the custody of soldiers assigned by Maj. Gen. Kenyon B. Joyce, commanding general of the Northwest sector, and removed to Owens River Valley, Cal., after being fingerprinted and medically examined.

274 Involved

I. Nagatani, chairman for Bainbridge Island, for the Japanese-American Citizens' League, said there are 43 Japanese families on the island, totaling 274 persons; 83 of these foreign born. James Y. Sakamoto, Seattle Japanese citizens' spokesman, said he was surprised to hear the Japanese will be taken to California. He said he had believed they would be kept somewhere in the northwest.

Nagatani said the Bainbridge

(Continued on Page 2)

Western Defense Command and Fourth Army
Wartime Civil Control Administration

INSTRUCTIONS TO ALL
JAPANESE
Living on Bainbridge Island

All Japanese persons, both alien and non-alien, will be evacuated from this area by twelve noon Monday, March 30, 1942.

No Japanese person will be permitted to leave or enter Bainbridge Island after 9:00 a. m. March 24, 1942, without obtaining special permission from the Civil Control Office established on this island near the ferry boat landing at the Anderson Dock Store in Winslow.

The Civil Control Office is equipped to assist the Japanese population affected by this evacuation in the following ways:

1. Give advice and instructions on the evacuation.
2. Provide services with respect to the management, leasing, sale, storage or other disposition of most kinds of property, including: farms, livestock and farm equipment, boats, tools, household goods, automobiles, etc.
3. Provide temporary residence for all Japanese in family groups, as specified below.
4. Transport persons and a limited amount of clothing and equipment to their new residence, as specified below.
5. Give medical examinations and make provision for all invalided persons affected by the evacuation order.
6. Give special permission to individuals and families who are able to leave the area and proceed to an approved destination of their own choosing on or prior to March 29, 1942.

The following instructions must be observed:

1. A responsible member of each family, preferably the head of the family, or the person in whose name most of the property is held, and each individual living alone, will report to the Civil Control Office to receive further instruction. This must be done between 8:00 a. m. and 5:00 p. m. Wednesday, March 25, 1942.

2. Before leaving the area all persons will be given a medical examination. For this purpose all members of the family should be present at the same time, when directed by the Civil Control Office.

3. Under special conditions, individuals and families will be permitted to leave the area prior to the date for complete evacuation indicated above. In general, the conditions imposed on voluntary evacuation are as follows: (a) That the destination be outside of Military Area No. 1, prescribed by Proclamation No. 1 of the Commanding General, Western Defense Command and Fourth Army, March 2, 1942; (b) That arrangements have been made for employment and shelter at the destination.

4. Provisions have been made to give temporary residence in a reception center elsewhere. Evacuees who do not go to an approved destination of their own choice, but who go to a reception center under Government supervision, must carry with them the following property, not exceeding that which can be carried by the family or the individual:
   (a) Blankets and linens for each member of the family;
   (b) Toilet articles for each member of the family;
   (c) Clothing for each member of the family;
   (d) Sufficient knives, forks, spoons, plates, bowls and cups for each member of the family;
   (e) All items carried will be securely packaged, tied and plainly marked with the name of the owner and numbered in accordance with instructions received at the Civil Control Office.
   (f) No contraband items may be carried.

5. The United States Government through its agencies will provide for the storage at the sole risk of the owner of only the more substantial household items, such as iceboxes, washing machines, pianos and other heavy furniture. Cooking utensils and other small items must be crated, packed and plainly marked, with the name and address of the owner. Only one name and address will be used by a given family.

6. Each family, and individual living alone, who goes to a reception center will be furnished transportation and food for the trip. Transportation by private means will not be permitted. Instructions will be given by the Civil Control Office as to when evacuees must be fully prepared to travel.

**Go to the Civil Control Office at the Anderson Dock Store in Winslow
between 8:00 A. M. and 5:00 P. M. on March 25, 1942,
to receive further instructions.**

J. L. DeWITT
Lieutenant General, U. S. Army
Commanding

the men, saying, "Sir, we'll be happy to show you where best to post your notices," the *Review* reported. Thus began one of the more poignant aspects of the exclusion process as the young soldiers from New Jersey, always professional in carrying out their orders, gradually began to realize the full impact of what they had been called upon to do.

Many who have since lived through decades of civil rights protests may wonder at the Nikkei's dutiful acceptance of this encroachment on their citizenship rights. Nagatani said years later, "It may sound crazy to you, but you've never lived through those times. People didn't question the government back then." The Nisei in particular wanted desperately to demonstrate their loyalty. In addition, Walt noted, "You don't argue with the army in time of war." Nagatani agreed: "How do 272 Japanese on the Island fight a company of army soldiers?"

Fumiko Nishinaka Hayashida feared primarily for her young children's rights. "You do what they want you to do, especially when your children are young," she said in a 2006 BIJAC oral history. "I was afraid that they might [take away their] citizenship."

Recognizing the futility of resistance in a climate of heightened wartime tensions, Milly explained in 1983, "They would have been forced to go." She also observed that refusing to comply would not have been the Japanese way. "It's not in their bringing up. I don't say it's not their nature, because natures are all the same really. But it's the way you've been brought up. And the Japanese were brought up to be docile and obedient and cheerful."

With the posting of Civilian Exclusion Order No. 1, it was official. DeWitt's directive ordered "all persons of Japanese ancestry, including aliens and non-aliens, be excluded from that portion of Military Area No. 1, described as 'Bainbridge Island'" on or before noon on March 30. Bainbridge Island was to be first. Both aliens and "non-aliens"—a euphemism for "citizens" worthy of George Orwell's *1984*—were included. What's more, the exclusion was to happen in just six days. Six days to make arrangements for houses, businesses, belongings, and pets. Six days to prepare to leave home for an undetermined length of time.

Walt and Milly indignantly responded to the order with a front-page editorial in the next edition two days later.

> But we are talking here about 191 AMERICAN CITIZENS! Where, in the face of their fine record since December 7, in the face of their rights of citizenship, in the face of their own relatives being drafted and enlisting in our Army, in the face of American decency, is there any excuse for this high-handed, much-too-short evacuation order?

The six preparation days are remembered only vaguely by local Nikkei. "I don't know if we slept very much or not, knowing that we were going to be leaving," recalled Kay Nakao. They knew very little about what was to happen. Where were they going? How long would they be gone? What should they pack?

"I had a little suitcase which I really stuffed," recalled Nobi Omoto. "And then I had a little shopping bag, stuffed. And a couple of school books. And then I put layers and layers of clothes on."

Shigeko Nishinaka Kitamoto, Fumiko's sister, whose husband had been arrested by the FBI and was interned at Fort Missoula, faced the evacuation with four young children, including her infant daughter, Chiseko "Jane." Like many other Island farmers, she entrusted her farm to one of her workers, Felix Narte, who agreed to care for the family home and farmland. Narte, who had emigrated from the Philippines in the 1920s, had previously worked for her parents.

All across the Island, hurried arrangements were also made between the Nikkei and their Caucasian neighbors. Ken Myers, going against specific company instructions, made sure his clients had proper insurance coverage. Clark Burkheimer provided essential legal advice to Nikkei families. Orville Robertson of the Society of Friends agreed to look after some of the less-established farms, thus preserving ownership for the Nikkei. Arnold Raber bought the Kouras' farm for one dollar and promised to resell it to them for that price upon their return.

Despite what it meant for them, many of the Island Nikkei, opposite top, such as (from right to left) George "Joe" Chihara, Robert Koba, Takashi Sakuma, and an unidentified Issei, helped the soldiers that had come to post Civilian Exclusion Order No. 1, opposite bottom. Below: The order gave the Islanders only six days in which to prepare for their removal.

Butcher and Preacher---All Japanese Must Leave Bainbridge Island Homes

Reach All for Christ

HIS CHURCH MUST CLOSE—Kihachi Hirakawa, elderly pastor of Winslow's Japanese Baptist Church, shown at the altar of the little mission he built forty-one years ago with his own labor.

OUT OF BUSINESS SOON—Johnny Nakata, meat and grocery merchant at Winslow, on Bainbridge Island, shown waiting on the trade. He's trying to get someone to take over his interests while he's gone under army evacuation orders.

Liberty, Justice Denied: Executive Order 9066

On February 19, 1942, President Franklin D. Roosevelt perpetrated what the American Civil Liberties Union has called "the worst single wholesale violation of civil rights in our history" when he signed Executive Order 9066. The order sanctioned the military to circumvent the constitutional protections of American citizens, effectively transferring control of civilians from the Justice Department to the Department of War and the army without a declaration of martial law. As a result of that order, nearly 120,000 persons of Japanese descent, half of them children, two-thirds of them American citizens, were forced—without criminal charges or due process hearings—to leave their West Coast homes and businesses to spend the duration of the war in what FDR called "concentration camps."

Conditions in the camps were primitive. Barbed wire separated the inmates from the rest of America. Armed guards in watchtowers loomed over tar-papered wooden barracks that housed entire families in single rooms, each with one lone hanging light bulb for illumination and wire cots for beds. The camps were demoralizing and desolate, located in arid and bleak areas where the weather was often extreme. Toilets, showers, and dining areas were communal; privacy was almost nonexistent.

This forced migration was justified at the time as protection against sabotage and espionage, although in 1976 author Michi Weglyn documented in *Years of Infamy: The Untold Story of America's Concentration Camps* that "our government had in its possession proof that not one Japanese American, citizen or not, had engaged in espionage, not one had committed any act of sabotage." None of those incarcerated was ever charged with, let alone convicted of, such crimes.

A majority lost everything they had before the war: homes, businesses, farms. Loss estimates vary, but it is clear that property and possessions worth many millions were lost by Japanese Americans during World War II. When the camps were eventually closed in 1946, the Nikkei were given $25 and one-way transportation fare and simply released. No attempt was made to reestablish the Nikkei in their former homes. Many of the elderly Issei, prevented by law from becoming naturalized citizens, had lived in the U.S. since the turn of the twentieth century. They had nowhere to go and were left with nothing.

Although the United States had three foes in World War II, only American citizens of Japanese descent were confined in this manner. Fewer than three hundred German and Italian Americans were individually arrested and, after judicial hearings, excluded from coastal areas. Also, quite significantly, most of the 150,000 Nikkei living in Hawaii, three thousand miles closer to the enemy, were not arrested or confined; the incarceration of Hawaiian Japanese would have devastated the territory's economy. E.O. 9066 only affected Japanese Americans—most of them successful farmers—on the West Coast.

The United States has since recognized and admitted that the wartime incarceration was a monumental error. President Gerald Ford repealed E. O.

9066 in 1976 on the thirty-fourth anniversary of its signing, saying its enactment was "a very, very sad day in American history." He further called upon the American people "to affirm with me the unhyphenated American promise that we have learned from the tragedy of that long ago experience . . . and resolve that this kind of error shall never be made again."

President Jimmy Carter signed legislation creating the Commission on Wartime Relocation and Internment of Civilians (CWRIC) in 1980 to study the effects of E.O. 9066. In its report, *Personal Justice Denied*, the independent, bipartisan commission stated its conclusions: the incarceration of Japanese Americans had not been justified by military necessity, nor was it founded upon military considerations, but rather was the result of "race prejudice, war hysteria, and a failure of political leadership."

Calling it "a grave personal injustice," the CWRIC report noted the extensive negative effects on the lives of "the excluded people." Losses to income and property were estimated to be as high as $2 billion in 1983 dollars, not counting "job training, education, and the like." It noted, "Less tangibly, the ethnic Japanese suffered the injury of unjustified stigma that marked the excluded." The report spoke of physical and psychological pain and deprivation of a traditionally close family structure.

The commission grappled with the issue of redress. After years "behind the barbed-wire of a relocation camp, branded potentially disloyal because of one's ethnicity alone—these injustices cannot neatly be translated into dollars and cents. History cannot be undone; anything we do now must inevitably be an expression of regret and affirmation of our better values as a nation, not an accounting which balances or erases the event of the war. That is now beyond anyone's power. It is well within our power, however, to provide remedies for violations of our own laws and principles. This is one important reason for the several forms of redress recommended. . . . Another is that . . . nations that forget or ignore injustices are more likely to repeat them."

Following the recommendations of the commission, Congress passed the Civil Liberties Act of 1988. When President Ronald Reagan signed it into law, he formally apologized on behalf of the United States to Japanese Americans for this "grave wrong," saying, "We must recognize that the internment of Japanese-Americans was . . . a mistake."

Implementing directives from Congress, presidents George H. W. Bush and Bill Clinton sent redress payments to the surviving inmates. In his accompanying letter, Clinton offered "a sincere apology . . . for the actions that unfairly denied Japanese Americans and their families fundamental liberties during World War II."

The signing of Executive Order 9066, which led to the posting of the Civilian Exclusion Order No. 1, opposite, was repealed by President Gerald Ford in 1976. Below: The proclamation signed by President Ford officially declaring that E.O. 9066 was terminated at the end of World War II, and the pen with which he signed his "American Promise."

As army officials notified Islanders of the March 30 evacuation date, the Nisei remained cooperative in the face of ever-changing instructions. Because of the Nisei's ability to speak English, the responsibility of working with the army fell mostly on the second generation despite their youth. Here, a group of Nisei discuss with soldiers the locations where the exclusion orders would be posted.

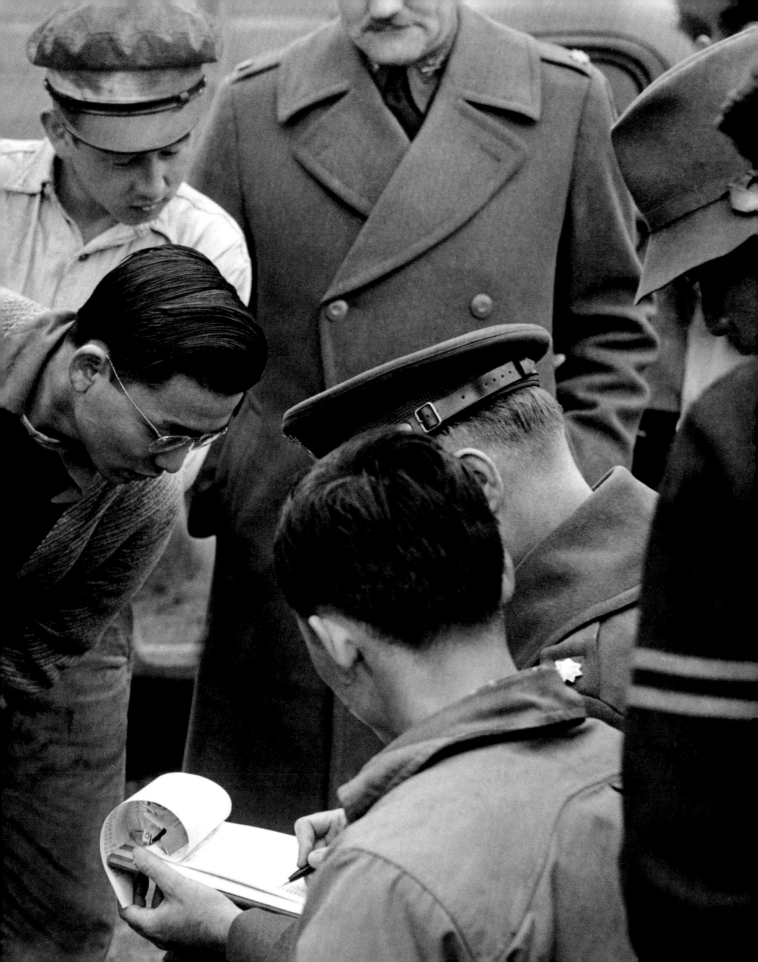

Eve Bucklin stored the Sakais' rugs. The Schmidts took care of the Hayashidas' dishes. The Hydes assisted the Nishimoris. The Burnses helped the Suyematsus. *Hakujin* (Caucasian) customers settled tabs with grocer Masaaki "Johnny" Nakata over his protests, saying, "You'll need this." In 1983 Hatsuko Koura commented on that neighborly concern, remembering, "The closeness of Bainbridge Islanders has been incredible. Other areas aren't that way, not as friendly and close."

The list of neighbors who helped at that crucial time is long: Jack Marshall, Mrs. Osgood, the Cumles, the Tarabochias, the Caves, the Loveriches, Hjalmer Anderson, the Flodins, the Yennes, and many others. Such widespread assistance was not common in most communities facing the exclusion. Fumiko Hayashida explained, "Bainbridge is close knit; everybody's interested, including *hakujin*."

The young people especially remembered the many kindnesses shown by teachers and school administrators. Teacher Ellen Hefner gave Hisa Hayashida Matsudaira, one of her kindergarten students, a picture of herself and copies of *The House That Jack Built* and *Raggedy Ann and Andy*, which "I memorized and brought home with me [from camp]," Matsudaira recalled. Fourth grader Shimako "Sally" Nishimori Kitano remembered, "Our principal talked to all of us who were to be interned" and expressed his sorrow. "My teacher, Miss Saari, was very kind and wished me well."

The high school faced a tremendous loss. Nearly a quarter of its students, including many class leaders, top scholars, and star athletes, were forced to withdraw seven weeks before the end of term. On December 8, Superintendent Phil Ruidl had joined Principal Roy Dennis and teachers in an assembly that mirrored the *Review's* call for calm. When the exclusion began, teacher Statira Biggs arranged for those remaining to correspond with those leaving.

Ikuko "Iku" Amatatsu Watanabe, senior class treasurer, said, "Mr. Dennis asked the government for permission for us to attend the Senior Ball and the Senior Sneak." Milly joined Dennis in asking that the curfew be extended for the thirteen seniors, but they were both denied.

One of the most heartfelt and dramatic expressions of support came as Bainbridge High School faced rival North Kitsap in the Tri-County baseball opener. Three days before their evacuation, Coach Walt "Pop" Miller sent all six Nisei players onto the field—and kept them there. With some of his star players on the bench, the competitive coach let his team fall 15–2 because "he just wanted all of the Japanese Americans to play their last game for Bainbridge and enjoy themselves," said center fielder Paul Ohtaki. "I will be eternally grateful to Pop Miller for letting all of us . . . play . . . regardless of how good we were."

During the hurried six days before evacuation, Milly and Walt had promoted their young janitor to camp correspondent—with a boost in pay to $5.50 a month. Ohtaki was a shy, quiet teenager unsure of his writing

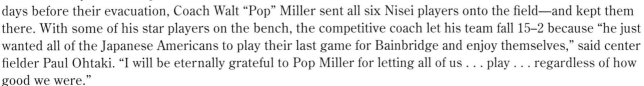

In the days leading up to their exile, Island Nikkei were helped by neighbors as they scrambled to prepare. Above: BHS Principal R. G. Dennis helped students transfer credits to the school at Manzanar. Opposite top: Neighbors helped Henry Takayoshi and his sons, Takato and Ben, pack their belongings. Opposite bottom: Tea cups from the Japanese Hall, a social gathering place for Nikkei before the war.

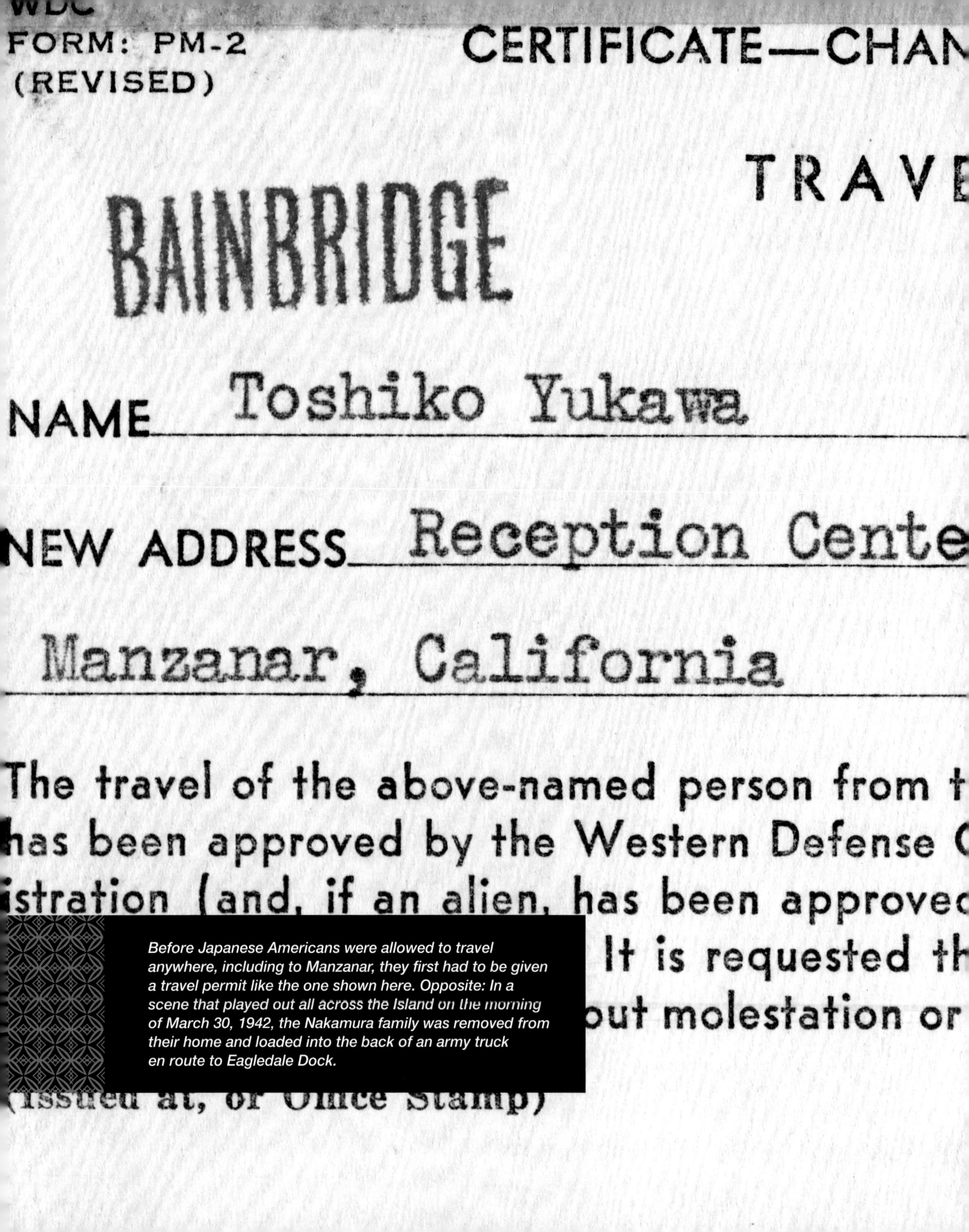
WDC
FORM: PM-2
(REVISED)

CERTIFICATE—CHAN

TRAVE

BAINBRIDGE

NAME Toshiko Yukawa

NEW ADDRESS Reception Cente

Manzanar, California

The travel of the above-named person from t
has been approved by the Western Defense C
istration (and, if an alien, has been approvec
It is requested th
out molestation or

(Issued at, or Office Stamp)

Before Japanese Americans were allowed to travel anywhere, including to Manzanar, they first had to be given a travel permit like the one shown here. Opposite: In a scene that played out all across the Island on the morning of March 30, 1942, the Nakamura family was removed from their home and loaded into the back of an army truck en route to Eagledale Dock.

ability. He reluctantly agreed to
be their reporter only when they
told him they'd "fix it up" if he
would "just write as if you were
talking to us." As Walt and Milly
said, it was important that "births,
deaths, who got married, who is
playing first base on the baseball
team . . . the usual news of a small
community" be in the *Review* from
the camp every week. That way, the
couple reasoned, other Islanders
could keep up on the news of their
"neighbors who are away for a
while." Walt later explained to Paul
in a letter,

When this mess is all
over, you people are
going to want to come home. You'll be welcomed with open arms by the vast majority of us. But those who
don't or won't understand . . . may actually try to stir up trouble.

But they'll have a hell of a hard time of it if, in the meantime, you've been creating the impression that the
Japanese are just down there for a short while and that . . . they still consider the Island as their home. Any and
every scrap of stuff you can gather about how they miss the Island is fuel for the fire. See what I mean?

"It is hard to believe the foresight Walt and Mildred Woodward had in coming up with a plan that early,"
Ohtaki wrote in his 2001 essay. "While we were making our plans for the evacuation . . . the Woodwards were
. . . making plans [to] smooth our return home."

Evacuation day came all too soon for such preparations, final school events, and good-byes. On the morning of
March 30, 1942, large army trucks lumbered up Island driveways to pick up family groups and transport them to
the ferry *Kehloken*. It would sail to Seattle and deliver them to a waiting train.

Leaving their new home, Hatsuko Koura watched her ailing father, sixty-eight-year-old Nobuzo, who was weak
from asthma, gaze at his berry fields framed by the majestic Olympic Mountains beyond: "[He] was lying down,
raised his head, and looked all around and lay down again . . . [sensing] he'll never see his home again."

Fumiko Hayashida, pregnant and with two small children, remembered the jumble of that "sad day . . .
scary day" when she "left everything." She had been assured by the county sheriff just days earlier that any
attempt to remove her family from their home would be unlawful. Now, fully outfitted soldiers were escorting
her away from her home. "We were really careful," she said in 2006. "We were prisoners . . . [and] they had
guns with the spears."

The Power of the Press

Japanese immigrants and Japanese American citizens "must not be made to suffer for the sins of a government . . . for whom they have no . . . allegiance," the *San Francisco News* asserted after Pearl Harbor. The *San Francisco Chronicle* said, "Americans called them Japanese, though the great majority of them have every right to be called Americans." The *Kent News-Journal*, from a Puget Sound community not unlike Bainbridge Island, stressed the loyalty of its Japanese citizens.

Many West Coast newspapers like these joined the *Bainbridge Review* in calling for calm in early December 1941. The tenor of most articles was fair, calling for all "enemy aliens" to be treated the same. Few news stories mentioned incarceration.

Even in the first week of February 1942, the *San Francisco Chronicle* did not detect any public outcry and bluntly suggested that certain politicians and journalists were manipulating public opinion. "The supposed 'hysteria' over enemy aliens and their descendants scarcely exists among the people themselves," the paper wrote. "The excitement is visible almost entirely in political and journalistic quarters. . . . They are seeking to capitalize on the supposed excitement of others, which is mostly a figment of their own imaginations."

As February progressed, however, most newspapers voicing opinions began calling for the Nikkei's removal. This nearly uniform call for banishment came in response to the demands of politicians, interest groups, and commentators with established anti-Japanese bias.

On December 30, 1941, after a thirty-six-hour visit to Pearl Harbor, Secretary of the Navy Frank Knox had released a statement claiming the attack on Hawaii was aided by "the most effective fifth column activity since Norway." Although quickly denied by the FBI and Hawaiian officials, it was Knox's statements—not the denials—that were widely covered by the media.

From that point on, media pressure for evacuation grew steadily. It increased after January 25, when Supreme Court Justice Owen Roberts, appointed by President Roosevelt to head a commission investigating the attack on Pearl Harbor, released his report and joined Knox in suggesting that the raid was abetted by Japanese Americans. "The press and radio played up these official announcements and spread false and foolish rumors," wrote noted historian Roger Daniels in *Prisoners Without Trial: Japanese Americans in World War II.*

Some papers, like the *Los Angeles Times* and the Northwest's *Bellevue American*, had targeted the Nikkei from the start, with the *Times* describing a "zone of danger" on the West Coast, one rife with Japanese "saboteurs and fifth columnists." Also weighing in early were such demagogues as widely syndicated Hearst columnist Henry McLemore, who stated, "I am for the immediate removal of every Japanese. . . . Personally I hate the Japanese and that goes for all of them." Another, John B. Hughes of the Mutual Broadcasting Company, asserted that Japanese residents on the West Coast were engaged in espionage and were controlling food supplies as part of a master war plan.

Walter Lippmann, a nationally known, widely respected liberal columnist, joined these less-revered pundits in early February and repeated the disputed reports from Hawaii. With convoluted logic, he suggested that the lack of any evidence of Japanese American disloyalty was in itself suspicious: "It is . . . a fact that . . . there has been no important sabotage on the Pacific Coast. . . . This is not . . . a sign that there is nothing to be feared. It is a sign that the blow is well-organized and that it is held back until it can be struck with maximum effect."

Westbrook Pegler, a popular and increasingly strident right-wing columnist, glad to gain legitimacy by association with Lippmann, added the Constitution to the argument, writing, "Do you get what [Lippmann] says? . . . The Japs ashore are communicating with the enemy offshore. . . . The Japanese in California should be under armed guard to the last man and woman right now and to hell with *habeas corpus* until the danger is over."

Not everyone agreed. Attorney General Francis Biddle wrote a memo to Roosevelt criticizing certain journalists. He evoked revered Supreme Court Justice Oliver Wendell Holmes Jr.'s 1919 decision on free speech, stating, "It is extremely dangerous for the columnists, acting as 'Armchair Strategists and Junior G-Men' to suggest that an attack . . . and planned sabotage is imminent. . . . It comes close to shouting FIRE! in the theater." Lippmann was singled out for Biddle's particular scorn: "Either Lippman [sic] has information which the War Department and the F.B.I. apparently do not have, or is acting with dangerous irresponsibility." His comments had little effect on Roosevelt's actions.

The clamor for exclusion, fueled by racial hatred and fear, was now prominent in West Coast newspapers. Joining the vitriolic comments of the *Los Angeles Times* were the two San Francisco papers and the *Sacramento Bee*, whose bigoted diatribes about Japanese went back to the turn of the century.

In the Northwest, the *Seattle Post-Intelligencer* and the *Seattle Times* both advocated the exclusion, as did the *Everett Herald*, the *West Seattle Herald*, the *Renton Chronicle,* and the *Sumner Standard*. The comments varied from the sensational to the sedate, but all blamed the Nikkei and favored their removal.

Even Edward R. Murrow, described by Daniels to be "as close to a patron saint as American journalism has produced," succumbed: "I think it's probable that, if Seattle ever does get bombed, you will . . . see some University of Washington sweaters on the boys doing the bombing!"

Protecting the West Coast from a well-organized attack from the Japanese American population was not the only argument made in the press for their removal. The protection of the Nikkei from fellow citizens seeking revenge for the bombing of Pearl Harbor or from racial tensions was also used as justification, below.

A Symbol of Safety
PROTECTION---NOT PERSECUTION

NEW HOME AHEAD FOR JAPANESE YOUNGSTER
UNDAUNTED YOUTH—Two-and-a-half-year-old Masura Shibayama, facing evacuation from Bainbridge Island with his parents, displays only polite interest in the sentry's fixed bayonet—he knows it isn't meant for him. (Story on Page 3.)

NAME **ICHIRO NAGATANI**

No. B-001

RETAINED BY PERSON TO WHOM ISSUED

News reports described the scene: soldiers, with bayonets fixed, lined the dock as families walked resolutely toward the ferry. Two hundred twenty-seven Islanders took that long walk down Lower Road (now Taylor Avenue). Captured in news photographs, the faces of young Japanese children registered confusion and fear, while their elders exhibited composure and dignity.

High school students were allowed to miss class to witness their friends' leaving. Some younger students came even without permission. "There were tearful farewells, hugs, and kisses, just like any kids being separated," Milly remembered. "It didn't make any difference which race was which."

With friends crowding the area, at some point they were confined to the field above the ferry dock. "[I]t kind of came as a shock to all of us," recalled Earl Hanson, a 1941 BHS graduate. He had told his employer, "I'm going to take time off. You can dock me whatever you want, but I'm going to see my Japanese friends off." When he got to Eagledale Dock, he was sent with other onlookers to an area too far away to speak with the exiles. He told one soldier, "You're taking away some of our best friends."

A soldier held eight-year-old Setsuko Kino while they awaited the ferry Kehloken. It was clear to everyone on the Island that the soldiers from New Jersey such as the two who led Ume and Yosuke Moji, opposite top, from their homes were polite and understood the gravity of the event. Below opposite: An identification tag similar to the one worn by all Nikkei on evacuation day.

On the other side of the barrier, Hanson's close friend Jerry Nakata was also shocked by the separation. "It was an odd feeling, you know. You leave your friends, and you lose your freedom," he said in a 2007 interview. "I didn't know who was there because there was a barricade. We couldn't even shake hands to say good-bye."

BHS student Margaret Copp Englund, who had "started in the first grade with nineteen Japanese children and twelve Caucasians," watched as her good friends since childhood were "being herded—herded—on the ferry."

Nakata, like several others, wore his BHS letterman's sweater that day. He remembered watching his father "on the upper deck, alone, with tears in his eyes, as if wondering, 'Will I ever see Bainbridge again?'" In boarding the *Kehloken,* Nakata's parents, Jitsuzo and Shima, carried a sign in recognition of an older son, Momoichi "Mo," who was serving in the U.S. Army.

Perhaps the most wrenching farewell was that of Ebaristo Arota and his wife, Miki. Because Ebaristo was a Filipino, he was forced to separate from his wife for the duration of the war, even though he had volunteered to join her in incarceration.

In the wheelhouse of the *Kehloken,* Captain Cyprian Wyatt turned the wheel over to a subordinate and said, "Watch her close. I'm going to go below and say good-bye to my friends." On his return, he offered the same opportunity to seaman Gordy Durrell, who accepted. "And I'm sorry I did," said Durrell, "because when I came back up, I was crying and so was Captain Wyatt!"

In Seattle, hundreds of people crowded onto an overpass to witness the Islanders exit the ferry and be led to the waiting train. It was, said Sam Nakao, "one of the most humiliating experiences I've ever gone through."

Some Island students, not content with their Bainbridge farewell, had taken the regular ferry

to the city to see their friends depart. Walt Woodward joined them to cover the departure for the *Review*. "[W]e spotted them and ran after the train, and we were all crying and waving good-bye to them," recalled Rich Barr, who would later serve as a paratrooper in the Pacific. "I fought the Japanese," he said, "but these kids here are still my real good friends, and they always were."

As soldiers marched the families down the dock to the waiting ferry, opposite, scores of friends and neighbors came to see them off. Above: Sisters Sachiko Koura Nakata (left) and Sumiko Koura Furuta watched their Island home disappear into the distance from the ferry Kehloken on its way to Seattle. In Seattle, they, along with the other Island Nikkei, would be herded onto trains bound for Manzanar.

According to Durrell, the soldiers assigned to oversee the transport made the same distinction Barr had. "[T]he soldiers were very kind to the Japanese," Durrell said. "A lot of the Japanese had enough [family] to carry what little they had. But some of them didn't. And those guys with the bayonets would help." Walt noted how affected the soldiers were by their task. "The soldiers were the ones that were crying. They knew finally what they really were doing and it just got to them."

The Southern Pacific Lines train, its seven cars filled exclusively with Bainbridge Islanders, headed south from Seattle. Although unknown to the passengers, its destination was a California desert valley. As it left the city, officers commanded that the cars' shades be drawn "for our safety," recalled Kay Nakao.

When the Islanders left Seattle, they had no idea where they would end up. It wasn't until two days later, after crossing the Sierra Nevadas, that they caught their first glimpse of Manzanar—the camp in which they would spend the first months of their exile. They were greeted by the blowing sand of the California desert and the hurriedly constructed barracks that were to be their homes.

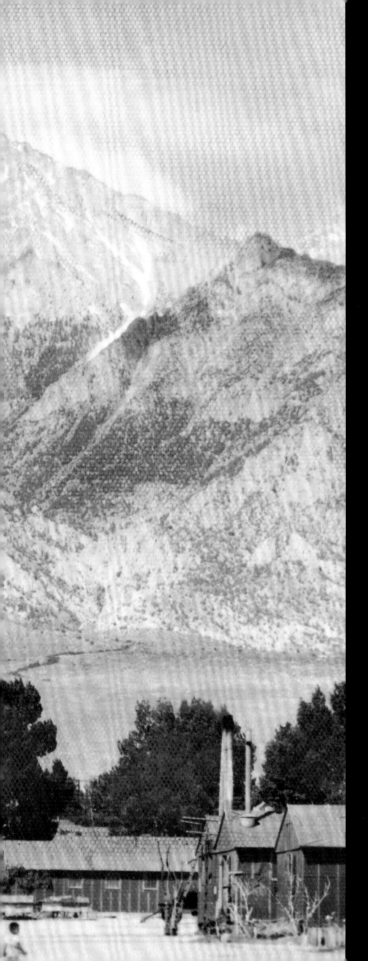

INCARCERATION

As the train pulled away from Seattle's waterfront, the apprehensive Islanders' sadness was lightened a bit by the heartfelt good nature of the young soldiers from New Jersey sent to escort them into exile. The children remembered with affection the tall smiling men who laughed and played games, while the young women remembered the soldiers' gentle concern and shy agreement to exchange letters, as Kay Sakai Nakao and Tony Ananzietta did. Thoughts of the Northwest's rugged Olympic and Cascade mountains surely came to mind as the train approached the Sierra Nevadas, but such thoughts would soon be

PARADISE LOST

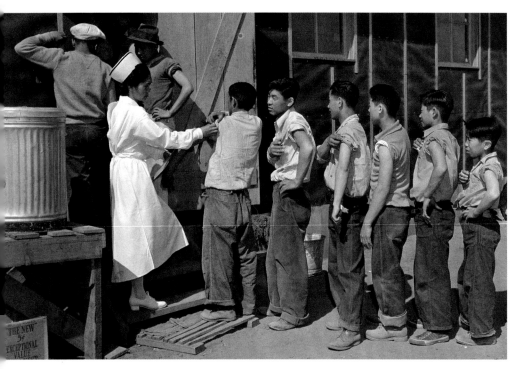

Upon their arrival at Manzanar, a group of Island Nisei, above, await vaccinations. While the Islanders acclimated to the camp, Walt and Milly were making plans to ease their eventual return. The couple had their camp reporters keep the population back home up to date with events such as the funeral of Nobuzo Koura, opposite top, and the wedding of Elise Amatatsu, opposite bottom, among many others.

vanquished as the exiles began the final leg of their journey. After two fitful nights on the train, the Islanders transferred to eight buses and headed up Route 395 into the Mojave Desert, where one recalled that "all we could see was sand with sagebrush and tumbleweed blowing in the wind on both sides." After a three-hour trek, the buses stopped. The Islanders got their first glimpse of their new home, the Manzanar War Relocation Center, with its row upon row of tar-papered barracks, most still under construction. The sight was heartbreaking. "Even some of the soldiers who escorted us down couldn't believe what they saw," said Paul Ohtaki. "Some had tears in their eyes as they left us."

Upon arrival, the Islanders were put to work stuffing straw into canvas ticks to make their own mattresses, which were placed on wire-spring cots. Each family was assigned a twenty-by-twenty-foot room, with four families per building.

Olive-drab army blankets and one small oil heater per room were intended to keep out the cold, but the buildings hardly stopped the desert from coming in. Green lumber was used for floorboards, and as it dried, the gaps became larger. "In the evening, the winds . . . would blow fine sand up through the floor cracks," Ohtaki said. "When we would get up each morning, we would have sand all over the place and all over our bodies."

Soon powerful searchlights would illuminate the camp day and night. Dining was in a common mess hall where, as Tatsukichi "Tats" Moritani recalled in 1987, "the first thing you [did] was turn the stack of bread over so that you wouldn't get a dusty piece." But, since everyone did this, it proved a futile exercise. Each block had its own latrines and showers, neither offering any privacy. Everywhere there were long lines. Mail was censored at times, and cameras were not allowed. Besides cots, no other furniture was supplied. If the inmates wanted such essentials as tables, chairs, or chests of drawers, they had to construct them from scrap lumber scavenged from camp construction sites.

News of their arrival was on the *Review*'s front page, above the fold, the next day. While that would not be remarkable in today's instant-news environment, in 1942 it was quite a feat, especially for a tiny weekly. Walt had made an agreement with one of the New Jersey soldiers to deliver Paul Ohtaki's account of the trip to the Associated Press for dispatch over its wire. His first report arrived just before the last press run.

Throughout the war, Ohtaki and three other young people, Sadayoshi "Sada" Omoto, Tony Koura, and Sachiko "Sa" Koura Nakata, faithfully documented the important events in the displaced Islanders' lives. When Fujiko Koba married Tadashi Sakuma in May 1942, Islanders learned that "[t]he bride wore a brown sport ensemble and matching accessories" and 175 friends enjoyed a four-layer cake at the reception. Friends commiserated when they learned Nobuzo "Grandpa" Koura was critically ill with pneumonia in mid-May, and shared the family's sorrow at the end of the month when they read of his funeral, attended by six pallbearers and some three hundred others. And under the headline "First Island Baby At Manzanar Born," those back home learned in August of the birth of Leonard, who would later become a popular Island school bus driver, to Mr. and Mrs. Saburo Hayashida of Island Center. Displaced Islanders were identified in the *Review* by their Island neighborhood, not as residents of Manzanar.

ELSIE AMATATSU WEDS DENVER MAN IN HUNT CEREMONY

By TONY KOURA
Review staff correspondent

● HUNT, Ida., Thursday, March 16—Elsie Amatatsu, daughter of Mr. and Mrs. Y. Amatatsu, Winslow, became the bride of Osamu Iwasaki, Denver, Colo., on March 4.

The bride was attired in the traditional white satin gown with fingertip veil and carried a bouquet of roses. Attending the bride as maid of honor was Kay Amatatsu, sister of the bride. Ikuko Amatatsu sang at the ceremony. She was here on a visit from Chicago, Ill.

* * *

A boy was born on February 28 to Mr. and Mrs. Tad Sakuma, Winslow.

* * *

Akio and Toshio Suyematsu, Port Madison, left recently for Ontario, Or., to do farm work.

* * *

Mr. and Mrs. Kumeo Tsubahara had a baby girl on March 4. She is the former Toshiko Katayama, daughter of Mr. and Mrs. I. Katayama, Winslow.

Anti-Japanese Furor

Those who blame the World War II incarceration of Nikkei on "war hysteria" should consider the roots of racism that run deep in American culture eventually to spring up in dialogue about citizens and immigrants of Japanese descent.

Immediately following the attack on Pearl Harbor, the conversation was measured and respectful. The day after the attack, Seattle mayor Earl Milliken called on citizens to be tolerant of Japanese Americans whom "we don't want to cut . . . adrift from us in this crisis." Two months later, however, Milliken advocated restrictions and said he was not willing to "take a chance on another Pearl Harbor."

Even Lieutenant General DeWitt, the man appointed to carry out the incarceration through Executive Order 9066, who would later declare, "The Japanese race is an enemy race," said in the early days of the war, "I'd . . . rather [not] attempt such wholesale internment. . . . An American citizen, after all, is an American citizen."

It wasn't long, however, before the various elements of historic anti-Japanese bias came together in an explosion of racism and greed that ultimately gave the military unprecedented authority over all civilians without a declaration of martial law. Building on decades of insidious bigotry against Asians, vocal politicians and military officers, together with members of the press and special interest groups, relentlessly played on wartime fears to create popular support for the exclusion.

Chinese immigrants in the 1800s were part of the West's rapidly expanding frontier society. Yet though the West was suddenly home to newcomers from many countries whose languages and customs were foreign to each other, it was the Chinese who were singled out for hostility and discrimination. Soon after their arrival, they were prohibited from testifying in court or voting. They faced a ceaseless barrage of violence and laws that refused them citizenship and land, culminating in the federal Chinese Exclusion Act of 1882, which barred immigration of Chinese laborers.

Japanese immigrants began arriving around 1870. At first, they were willing to take undesirable jobs for low pay, but they moved quickly into more skilled positions in agriculture, producing nearly 75 percent of western Washington's vegetables and most of its berries and small fruits prior to World War II. Fledgling labor unions, closed to Asians, saw them as competition and began lobbying for restrictions. Washington State's 1889 constitution barred Asians from owning land. The U.S. Supreme Court declared immigrants from Japan, like the Chinese, were "aliens ineligible for citizenship." Congress decreed that any woman marrying such an alien would lose her citizenship. In 1924, bowing to strong political pressure from the West Coast, the federal government stopped further immigration from Japan.

What began as a defense against economic competition had quickly taken on racial overtones. With widespread support on the West Coast, many politicians, white supremacists, newspaper publishers, and labor leaders played on people's fears of the unfamiliar by creating an enduring stereotype of the Japanese as sly, cunning, sinister, apelike creatures intent on domination.

Franklin D. Roosevelt was often open about his attitude toward Japanese Americans. In a 1925 newspaper column, the future president declared, "Japanese immigrants are not capable of assimilation into the American population." In 1936 as president, anticipating war with Japan, he suggested a plan in which "special intelligence files [would be] drawn up and concentration camps [would be] used to imprison Japanese Americans."

On December 15, 1941, after the Pearl Harbor attack and in what some historians have called a trial balloon for the exclusion, Mississippi representative John E. Rankin declared on the floor of the House of Representatives, "I'm for catching every Japanese in America, Alaska, and Hawaii now and putting them in concentration camps."

Earl Warren, a California gubernatorial candidate in 1942, warned in February: "There is no possible way of separating the loyal from the disloyal. . . . [D]ealing with the Caucasian race we have methods that will test the loyalty . . . but when we deal with the Japanese we . . . cannot form any opinion that we believe to be sound."

With surprising candor, Austin Anson of the Salinas Grower-Shippers admitted to economic reasons for wanting to exclude the Nikkei: "We've been charged with wanting to get rid of the Japs for selfish reason. We might as well be honest. We do. . . . And we don't want them back when the war ends, either."

Other officials opposed the exclusion, although not publicly. The Federal Bureau of Investigation had conducted inquiries of Japanese Americans for decades, and its director, J. Edgar Hoover, was convinced of their loyalty. In early February, he argued to FDR that the call for removal was not grounded in facts: "The necessity for mass evacuation is based primarily upon public and political pressures rather than on factual data. Public hysteria and . . . the comments of press and radio announcers are to blame."

But the racism of those like DeWitt carried the day. "A Jap's a Jap," said DeWitt. "They are a dangerous element . . . . It makes no difference whether he is an American: theoretically he is still a Japanese and you can't change him. . . . You can't change him by giving him a piece of paper."

Two months prior to Pearl Harbor, a State Department special investigator, Charles B. Munson, presented Roosevelt with a confidential report stating the Nikkei were of no danger to the nation. The FBI and navy intelligence corroborated Munson's findings in separate reports. In 1941, more than five months before the exclusion began, the U.S. government had plausible evidence exonerating the Nikkei of disloyalty. It did not release that information until 1946, a year after the war's end.

Those in the country calling for the removal of the Nikkei used long-held stereotypes and racist exaggerations to spread fear and hate to bolster their argument. One tool that borrowed heavily on these caricatures was the political cartoon, including the ones by Theodore Geisel, also known as Dr. Seuss, below, that appeared in the newspaper PM.

Walt and Milly realized the young staff correspondents' work would play a critical role in Bainbridge Island's reaction to the Nikkei exclusion. A twenty-first-century *Review* reporter, Dee Axelrod, summed up the couple's almost prescient understanding of the bigger picture. "Remarkably, [they] had not only grasped the full context of events that were just unfolding," wrote Axelrod, "but had also crafted a plan that would help reintegrate Japanese Americans into Bainbridge life—and Ohtaki was to play a key part in that scheme."

In the first weeks of April, Ohtaki was tentative about his assignment. He once sent a copy of the *Manzanar Free Press* in lieu of his column and received a tongue-lashing from Walt in return.

Milly and Walt also wrote frequent chatty letters of encouragement and friendship to their first reporter. Walt, who had a nickname for many of his friends, good-naturedly shared some reporter talk with Ohtaki, joking about his middle name:

> Dear Tsutomu: Now how do you pronounce THAT one? I've been trying for a week, but all I can get is ha-choo-moo. All of which sounds like the Empire Builder starting East for Chicago. . . .
>
> You're doing a fine job on the correspondence. That was [an] especially nice job you did on Mr. Koura's death. It caught us just in time to make a front-page bulletin. All of which was swell. We're sorry when any-body dies, of course. But a good newspaperman realizes that death is news—one of the top kind of news—and doesn't waste time on tears until he's turned in his yarn.

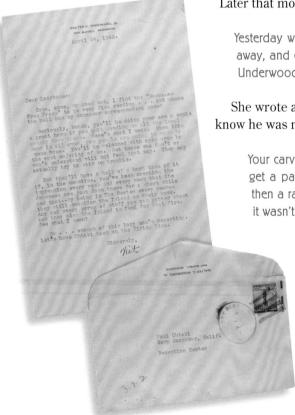

Later that month Milly sent a brief note of thanks to Ohtaki:

> Yesterday we finished the last of the rice you brought to us before you went away, and enjoyed it very much. How do you like this typewriter? It's the old Underwood that we used to think wouldn't work!

She wrote again in July, warmly thanking him for a gift he'd sent and letting him know he was missed:

> Your carvings are really cute, Paul, and it gave Carolyn Jane quite a thrill to get a package from you. We asked her if she remembered Paul. . . . Just then a rattly truck went by, and she said, "*That's* Paul?" But we assured her it wasn't Paul, unfortunately. We miss you around this place.

In October, Walt wrote to Ohtaki and his older brother, Peter, hoping to bolster their resolve:

> You fellows certainly have shown your true colors by your fine record at Manzanar. Don't let down for one second, no matter how bitter or dissolusioned [sic] you may feel. A real American just doesn't quit . . . ever.

With support from the Woodwards and their assurance that Islanders back home both needed and appreciated his work, the young reporter continued to record the lives of the exiled Islanders in the *Bainbridge Review*.

Kenneth Nakata, 16, Bainbridge High School sophomore, Winslow, and his two nephews, Donald, 7, and Wayne, 2, sons of Johnny [and Pauline] Nakata, former Winslow grocer[s], were chicken pox victims. . . .

Thirty-two Islanders, including eight girls, are contributing to the nation's war effort by working on the camouflage net project here. . . .

As the hot summer season progressed here this week, increasing numbers of Islanders, accustomed to the comparatively cool weather of their former sea-level homes, were complaining of sick headaches. . . . Island Japanese rejoiced with other residents here this week over announcement of a payscale. Salaries promised were $16 a month for professional and technical workers, $12 for skilled workers, and $8 for unskilled labor. . . . [This initial pay scale was changed to $19, $16, and $12, respectively.]

While those with subscriptions were able to get the Review, *the exiled Nikkei also had access to the* Manzanar Free Press, *below, a journal produced by a Japanese American staff and overseen by the camp directors. What started as a camp newsletter grew over its run to report on international, national, and camp news. Opposite: Walt explained to Ohtaki the importance of his reports in one of his frequent letters.*

Islanders learned when "Sachiko Koura, 17 years old, Manzanita, won third place in [the] Miss Manzanar beauty queen contest," a clear source of pride since "there are only 247 Bainbridge residents among the 10,000" at Manzanar. Two other teenagers got their names in print when the *Review* reported that "Pranksters daubed lipstick on the nose of Harry Koba, Winslow, while he slept," and "The lad who used to pay those overdue fees to Mrs. Gideon . . . is at it again; Shig Moritani's favorite hideout seems to be the Manzanar library."

Surely inspiring a few chuckles as well was the report of "a Bainbridge Island Japanese (he'd better remain anonymous)" who routinely defied the camp's ban on the traditional tub bath by "daily . . . trudg[ing] to the shower room, carrying his washtub, and scrub[bing] furiously in the tub under the shower sprinkler."

As the school year drew to a close, Bainbridge High School joined the *Review* in keeping the connection with the exiles alive. "Principal Roy G. Dennis was so wonderful that I named my first son, Dennis, after him," said Nobi Omoto in 2007.

Even though they were given very little to work with, the Nikkei transformed their dismal surroundings into a home of sorts. Whether it was by constructing furniture for their barracks or by transforming the desert landscape of Manzanar into an oasis of greenery and flowing water, they did their best to make the experience not only tolerable, but also, at times, a thing of beauty.

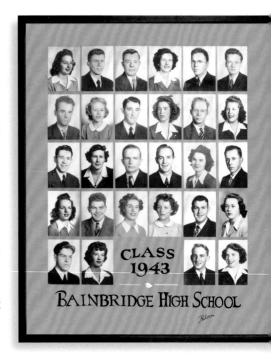

Thirteen copies of the school yearbook, *Spartan Life*, were circulated at the high school for student signatures. Their arrival in Manzanar elicited the same happy exchanges seen on countless high school campuses that June. Both Principal Dennis and Superintendent Ruidl mailed copies of their commencement addresses, which were read at the informal graduation gathering at Manzanar.

Nobi Omoto and the twelve other excluded members of the BHS Class of 1942 share bittersweet memories of what should have been the highlight of their young lives. Even with the school's efforts, the pain of not celebrating graduation day with the other thirty-nine students in their close-knit class was very real. "The day of Bainbridge's graduation, I felt so empty and sad, for after twelve years [of school] that day would have been very special," Omoto said in 2001. "I sat on my bunk and cried."

At graduation back home, thirteen chairs were left empty in poignant recognition of those friends prevented from attending. Omoto, a popular athlete and honor student at BHS in 1942, sent a congratulatory telegram to her classmates, which was read at the graduation ceremony in a moment of somber reflection.

All these graduation events were duly reported in the *Review*, as was that other sure sign of summer: baseball. On the Fourth of July, Jerry Nakata was leading "his baseball league in hitting last week, boasting an average of .500. Gerald [George] Okazaki and Nob Oyama, both of Winslow, also were hitting over the .300 mark." Not to be outdone by the boys, "the Bainbridge girls softball team . . . won their first game. . . . The chucker for the team, Mary Chihara, hurled a masterful game, winning a shut-out 29–0."

News from home of the once-promising strawberry crop, however, wasn't good. Expected in March to top $250,000, the crop was now failing due to "rain all the time except for one or two good, hot days" and too few pickers. Many workers had willingly traded the excruciating stoop labor of picking strawberries for shipyard work with its higher wages. While the berry crop at home was a loss because of their absence, many working-age exiled Islanders were employed through agricultural furloughs in the beet and potato fields of Idaho and Montana.

Even as the Islanders became more accustomed to Manzanar, they were always aware they were prisoners, confined with ten thousand others in one square mile of living space. At his sixtieth high school reunion, Sada Omoto, retired professor of art history at the University of Michigan, told his classmates that "Mr. Dwight Davis's civics class did not prepare me for Executive Order 9066." Omoto, who had been the 1941 senior class president, keenly felt the loss of freedom. Instead of seeing the lofty Sierra Nevadas in the distance, he could only "stare at the barbed wire which surrounded the camp." He told his classmates of "the monotonous buildings, the guard tower, the barbed wire fence, [and] the endless dust."

Unexpectedly, in early December 1942, tragedy struck at Manzanar. When a group of protesting prisoners failed to disburse, army guards opened fire. One prisoner was killed instantly, another died later, and nine others were wounded. Martial law was declared, a communications embargo was enacted, and the Island was

At the start of the school year, the Bainbridge Island High School class of 1942 was representative of the Island's diverse population. But by the time the class of 1943, opposite, graduated, the exclusion of the Japanese American students had clearly left its mark. Not only did the forced exile separate friends and classmates, it also stripped the school of one of its hallmarks—its diversity.

without its usual correspondent's report. The *Review* didn't go to press without news from the exiles, though. Milly and Walt told their readers the paper had "received reports from Islanders who said friends in Manzanar had written them declaring flatly that no Island Japanese participated in the riot."

In fact, the small group of Northwesterners had seemed mismatched with the rest of the Manzanar Nikkei from the very beginning, and the fatal confrontation highlighted the differences. These small-town Islanders had been transplanted into a community of ten thousand Californians, many of whom were city people. Hastily housed at Manzanar because it was the first facility available, the Bainbridge group had long wished to be closer to the others from Washington incarcerated at Minidoka, in southern Idaho.

Milly and Walt supported that wish in an editorial titled "You Shouldn't Pack Apples with Lemons," a reference to the primary farm crops of each state. They and other Islanders helped facilitate the transfer in letters to the War Relocation Authority. In March 1943, most of the Bainbridge group made the move in another long train ride, from Block 3 at Manzanar to Block 44 at Minidoka. They found similar extremes of weather and terrain, but also many old friends. The few who remained at Manzanar did so to be near California relatives.

The three Island families who had managed to escape incarceration by moving outside Military Area 1 to Moses Lake, Washington, before the travel ban went into effect remained there throughout the war. Zenji Shibayama, a sixteen-year-old sophomore in 1942, recalled in a 2006 interview how the group traveled across the Cascade Mountains in one of his grandfather's vans: "I remember we had a tough time because it was all loaded. Trying to go through the [mountain] pass we had radiator trouble. We had to melt snow [for] the radiator."

Although Shibayama doesn't recall having problems in Moses Lake, his younger cousin Junkoh Harui does. "I had very traumatic experiences in the school in Moses Lake when I first got there," recalled Harui in 2002. He received a daily beating from the same older boy, while curious youngsters looked on. "It took about a half a year or so for us to melt the people down," he said. "[Then] they discovered that we are good citizens and that we work hard and there's nothing to fear."

After reports came out about a disturbance at Manzanar, above top, it became evident that the Islanders shared little in common with their fellow exiles. The combined effort of editorials by Walt and Milly, above, and letters from the Islanders convinced the War Relocation Authority to allow the Islanders to move to Block 44 at Minidoka, opposite top. Opposite: Nobuichi Moritani's bag from the Idaho camp.

Harui's uncle, Zenmatsu Seko, who owned Bainbridge Gardens with Harui's father, Zenhichi, had been arrested by the FBI in February 1942 and was incarcerated at Fort Missoula, Montana. Even though the rest of the Harui family was spared confinement behind barbed wire, "we were still monitored," Harui said. "We had a gentleman that checked on us every month to . . . make sure we didn't have rifles or cameras or radios. . . . " The families, like those at Manzanar, were not free to return home.

The Islanders at Manzanar began to taste a bit of freedom by the summer of 1942, when the federal government began short-term agricultural leaves. By the next summer, individuals were allowed to relocate east of the Western Defense Command for jobs and school.

Paul Ohtaki took advantage of the program and, after a year as the *Review*'s staff correspondent, left in July 1943 for work in Chicago and then school at DePaul University. A year later, he volunteered as an interpreter for the army's Military Intelligence Service (MIS). After extensive training, he was stationed in the Philippines, processing and interrogating prisoners of war and civilians.

Ohtaki's departure meant the *Review* needed a new correspondent. Sada Omoto filled in briefly until he left for school at Oberlin College. He then followed Ohtaki to the Pacific with the MIS and completed his schooling after the war.

Surveillance and Arrests

"One of the Japanese aliens seized in a Federal Bureau of Investigation raid on Bainbridge Island last spring returned to his family at [Manzanar] last week," the *Review* reported on June 24, 1942. "The man, whose name was withheld, had not seen his family since the raid [on February 4, 1942]. He was released from a detention center in Missoula, Mont. Other Islanders still held are awaiting hearings."

Forty-two Issei Islanders had been taken into federal custody after the warrantless raids on Island Japanese homes two months after Pearl Harbor. Many were released after questioning, although thirteen were taken to the Dearborn Street offices of Seattle's Immigration and Naturalization Service. Eleven were subsequently transported to Justice Department internment camps.

A now unclassified confidential report from the Thirteenth Naval District's Intelligence Office offers insight into their arrests and internment. A 1942 "survey of Bainbridge Island, Washington, to determine the number of suspects living in the area" listed several investigated groups: alien employees at the Winslow shipyard, alien residents of the Island, "Japanese suspects," and "Filipino suspects." The report also included general suspect files divided into "Axis," "Communist," and "Miscellaneous." Walt Woodward is listed under Axis: "very friendly to Japanese . . . maintains editorial policy denouncing General DeWitt."

Comments about the Nikkei suspects included their leadership in various community organizations, activity in the local judo club and the Japanese language school, and possession of contraband. The "contraband" was dynamite, caps, and fuses, items historically used on Island farms.

Even routine Island life was labeled suspicious. The report describes the activity of Yoshito "Frank" Kitamoto, identified as an "enemy alien" by the FBI, who "was apprehended November 28, 1940, in company of two other Japanese 'gathering clams' on shore approach to Naval Radio Station." In 1940—more than a year before the U.S. declared war on Japan—digging clams was a routine chore for Islanders, and one would be hard pressed to find an Island beach that did not face a military installation.

The report also listed forty Island Filipinos who were helping Nikkei farmers and included an amplified list of six Filipinos and two "white residents of Bainbridge associated with Filipinos," one of whom is "reported sympathetic toward Japanese evacuees and corresponding with them." Various comments describe the Filipino farmers: "suspicious individual," "very intelligent Filipino," "associate of . . . a white man living with him," and "doubt exists he is actually a Filipino in view of Japanese appearance."

In addition to Walt, other suspects were Gyozo and Tora Ohtaki, instructors in the language school and parents of the *Review*'s correspondent Paul Ohtaki; Orville Robertson for his work with the Society of Friends and for "corresponding with Japanese at the Relocation Center": and Lambert Schuyler, described as a "militant economic theorist" and the author of *Think Fast, America.*

This detailed report from Naval Intelligence is but one example of the extensive information on Nikkei and their associates compiled by federal agencies beginning in the 1920s. As Tetsuden Kashima, professor of American Ethnic Studies at the University of Washington, described it, "rational deliberation," rather than any widespread mass hysteria, was an important impetus for the wartime incarceration and internment of Nikkei.

The extent of this in-depth research is illustrated in Ichiro Nagatani's comments about a secret his Issei father had shared with only two people. "Some thirty-three years after my father's arrival here, when he was being interrogated by the FBI in Seattle, he was stunned to learn that the FBI knew on what day, from which ship, and in what port he had 'jumped ship,' and the name of the person who befriended him," recalled Nagatani. "I wonder why the FBI, with such good case histories on Japanese aliens, was not able to simply round up . . . the supposed spies . . . and leave the rest of us [to live our lives in peace]."

The eleven Islanders joined 17,477 other Issei, including 178 from Seattle who were interned during the war. In total, nearly 32,000 enemy aliens were interned, according to Kashima's landmark book *Judgment Without Trial: Japanese American Imprisonment During World War II*. Of these, the greatest percentage were of Japanese ancestry (54.8 percent), while those of German and Italian descent, although from resident groups far larger than the Japanese nationals, composed 36.1 percent and 8.5 percent, respectively.

In contrast to the inmates of incarceration centers such as Manzanar, internees were allowed hearings—though without legal representation—to determine if they should remain confined, be paroled, or in some cases, be released. German and Italian aliens were allowed to return to their homes and families, although certain restrictions curtailed their coastal activities. Japanese aliens were also released to their families, but could not return to their homes and remained incarcerated throughout the war.

The Issei Islanders were interned in Justice Department camps at Fort Missoula; Fort Lincoln, North Dakota; Santa Fe, New Mexico; and a Livingston, Louisiana, army center. One of the men interned as an "enemy alien" (Kitamoto) was in fact an American citizen born in San Francisco, but he was unable to produce birth records because they had been destroyed in the 1906 earthquake. Most of the Islanders were released from internment to the camps in 1942 and 1943. One Islander could not rejoin his family until 1944. Another Islander was not released from confinement until after the internment camps had been shut down in 1945, months after the end of the war.

For the Hayashida family, below, the removal to Manzanar was difficult enough, but when the head of the family, Ichiro (right), was taken to Missoula, Montana, during the FBI raids, the added concern of when the family would see their father and husband again weighed heavily on them. Daughter Hisa was so frightened of her "criminal" father, she hid from him when he eventually joined his family at Manzanar.

With so many of the working-aged men leaving the camps for the military, jobs, or school, women, children, and the elderly made up the majority of Minidoka's population. Extended families, such as the Hayashidas and Arimas, seen here posing outside their barracks, pulled together as best they could to see themselves through the hard life the camp offered.

Tony Koura, a high school senior, became the *Review*'s next reporter. Immediately, he won praise from Milly and Walt for his good work:

> If your first sample is any indication of your ability as a reporter . . . you'll do! . . . It's an important job you're doing, far more important than just reporting a few deaths, weddings and what not. . . .

The Woodwards told Koura how his weekly news report reminded Islanders back home that they had some three hundred neighbors "living elsewhere just now." They also shared their concern that the continued releases from camp might jeopardize the weekly reports if they couldn't find young reporters to handle the job. They encouraged Koura to "keep it alive."

After a year on the job, Koura, like Ohtaki and Omoto before him, entered a Midwest college and then the Military Intelligence Service. He completed an accelerated program and was sent directly to occupied Japan and, later, Manchuria.

Frank Kitamoto (foreground) and Leonard (back, center), Neal (to right of Leonard), and Susan Hayashida played along the plank sidewalks of Minidoka, above. The children had few toys, except those that they were able to bring with them, like Hisa Matsudaira's jacks, below. Opposite: The debate about the future of the Island Nikkei was a common topic in the Review's *Open Forum.*

Before leaving for Chicago in March 1944, he passed the reins to his younger sister, Sa Koura Nakata, of Miss Manzanar fame. She began regularly reporting "hard" news in addition to the lighter fare of births and weddings. Since the army had reversed its earlier ban on accepting Nisei volunteers, many Islanders were now in the service, including her brother, Art, and her fiancé, Mo Nakata. These young men, serving with the 442nd Regimental Combat Team, saw fierce fighting in Italy and France. Both were among the first Island Nisei wounded, news which Nakata faithfully reported.

The incarcerated Bainbridge Islanders often corresponded with friends back home, although mail, both incoming and outgoing, risked censorship. Others continued to exchange Christmas cards and gifts on birthdays.

A few determined Islanders committed the time and expense involved in taking the arduous trip to the camps in order to talk with their friends in person. Perhaps the first was a missionary for the Seattle Japanese Baptist Church who had come to the Island every week to teach Sunday school. As the *Review* reported, "Miss Esther Mary McCullough, former teacher of the Winslow Baptist Church, paid a welcome surprise visit" in July 1942. Another visitor was Miss Statira Biggs, a favorite teacher among the teenagers, who spent three days visiting with her students at Minidoka and sharing their families' cramped quarters.

Felix Narte, manager of the Kitamotos' farm, visited with Shigeko Nishinaka Kitamoto and her husband, Frank, at Manzanar. "Especially glad to see him were the [four] Kitamoto children, to whom the evacuation still is a puzzle," said Ohtaki's report. Narte made a second trip a year later, this time bringing a washing machine, a welcome gift for a woman with two children still in diapers. Clear evidence of the affection the Kitamotos held for him can be seen in the formal family portrait, which includes Narte, taken in an Idaho photography studio.

Gertrude "Gert" and Arnold Raber recounted their visits in a letter to the editor. They traveled first to Montana, "visiting the Koura boys. . . . They were working in the beet field with several other Island boys." One reason for their trip not mentioned in their letter was to bring the Kouras their half of the proceeds from the year's berry crop. In eastern Washington, they "visited the Seko family at Moses Lake, who inquired about the Island folk and extended greetings."

Perhaps the most frequent traveler between Puget Sound and the incarcerated Islanders in Minidoka was not really a visitor to Idaho, but another transplant. The Reverand Emery Andrews of Seattle's Japanese Baptist Church had often brought his family to Bainbridge Island before the war to enjoy picnics in the company of their many Island friends. When the Northwest Nikkei were forced to leave and Andrews lost his congregation, he packed up his family and moved to Twin Falls. Undeterred by the displeasure of his denomination's national leadership and the discrimination and taunts he faced in Idaho, Andrews tirelessly served the inmates of Minidoka, completing fifty-six round-trips—about 1,500 miles each—to the Puget Sound area to pick up belongings and perform requested tasks.

THE OPEN FORUM

Editor, The Review:

My family and I are all for the attitude of your paper in regard to the Americans of Japanese ancestry. The editorial of the 10th is good. It is sane and reasonable and thoroughly American.

It is regrettable that the same can not be said for the action of the people who called the meeting and their sympathizers.

As I understand it, the F. B. I. has in custody all those known or suspected of subversive activities and we should have confidence in the ability of the F. B. I. Against the others there is no charge, no conviction; they therefore should be entirely free under the laws which protect all of us against idle charges.

It is sad to see, in these United States, folks imitating Mr. Schickelgruber, charging people with offenses because of the color of their skin, shape of the head, for having red hair or no hair.

Enclosed find $1.00, please send me some copies of the issue of the 10th which I would like to send to people who'd be interested.

HARRY M. MYERS,
Crystal Springs

HE OPEN FORUM

(Editor's note—Views expressed [in] this letter are not those of [th]e Review. For comment, see [edi]torial column.)

[Edi]tor, The Review:

[B]ainbridge Islanders are per[hap]s naturally friendly toward the nisei. We knew them as neighbors, the smiling and inscrutable [op]rators of truck farms and [groc]ery stores or as schoolmates [and] good sports. [A]nd our consti[tuti]on reminds us that we knew [som]e of them as fellow Ameri[cans] even though they may have monkey-jawed and yellow[skin]ed. We liked them and so we close our eyes and ears [our] minds to the reports of Jap [tre]atment of American prison[ers].

[But] others of us look upon all [that] the legal status of the nisei [notwiths]tanding, a little more in[telli]gently, if to be intelligent is [to be] self-interested. Legally and [as hu]man beings they have a [right] to return here when the war [is over]. But it was our ancestors, [not t]he were both white and [blac]k, who wrote that law, [our c]onstitution for the amend[ment of] which they made full pro[vision.] We propose to change it [with rega]rd to the Japs if only be[cause] they have proven them[selves] great deal less than hu[man in] the face of their barbar[ous treat]ment of our men on Ba[taan. We] don't want any Japs back [here.]

[W]e view this thing dispas[sionately]? Probably not. But we [must. W]hether nisei or not, [Japs who] return to Bainbridge will be met by insults and abuse, if not worse. Not as long as the youngest of them lives could he ever surmount the curse which has been laid upon his race. But if there were no curse, the Jap is not as[similable]. You would not have your daughter marry one; nor would you have your daughter ten times removed marry one that is only one-tenth Japanese. And because they are unassimilable as well as despised, to put it mildly, they will be unhappy, resentful, vengeful, even though legally they are full citizens. Perhaps because Americans are apt to over-do this fair-play business anyway, we might risk holding our own passions in check. But could we ever trust a Jap again? Could we put faith in people who know that they are despised?

The record of Jap subversive organizations as revealed by the Dies Committee bears out this point. Unless we are prepared to love and intermarry with the Japs we may expect more nisei to be traitors at heart.

As to "the battalion of them dying for America right now in Italy," death in modern war is not necessarily a matter of loyalty and self-sacrifice. Instead, it may be a case of being placed forcefully (the draft is not a polite invitation to serve) in a position of danger where one fights and dies because of a natural desire to go on living. Thus thousands of Italians died at the hands of Americans in Africa when they would have much preferred fighting on our side. Again, some of the best soldiers in history were quite indifferent to the cause for which they were supposed to be fighting.

No amount of star-spangled valor or on the part of conscripted Japs will change our minds. We don't want any Japs back here ever.

LAMBERT SCHUYLER
Winslow RFD

Filipino-Nikkei Friendships

The Kitamoto and Narte families have a special friendship that began a few years after Felix Narte arrived in this country in 1926 from the Philippines.

"Felix Narte—he was [my parents'] top hand—moved into this house and kept the farm going," recalled the Kitamotos' oldest daughter, Yuriko "Lilly" Kitamoto Kodama. "When we came back . . . my parents gave Felix part of their property."

Kodama's brother, Yoshikazu "Frank" Kitamoto, explained the significance of the Filipino Islander's help. "Just having the presence of people in their homes and looking after their property was important," explained Kitamoto, president of the Bainbridge Island Japanese American Community. Citing the damage done to unoccupied buildings like Bainbridge Gardens, whose greenhouses were destroyed and plants stolen, Kitamoto concluded, "If it weren't for these men of Filipino descent looking after the farms, it would have been very difficult for people to come back."

It was the support of *hakujin* friends and neighbors that created a welcoming climate on Bainbridge Island for the Nikkei. And it was the perseverance and hard work of Filipino farmhands that ensured they had something to return to.

Men from the Philippines, like eighteen-year-old Felix Narte, began arriving in the U.S. in the late 1920s just as the Great Depression made finding work difficult. Word of mouth brought several Filipino men to Bainbridge Island and its berry farms.

The work was hard and, perhaps because of the extreme economic situation, the men were not welcomed even to the degree that their Japanese predecessors had been. Doreen Almazan Rapada told an interviewer in 2007 something of what her father faced on Bainbridge: "There was a lot of prejudice. . . . They were called 'brown monkeys' and told to 'just go back where you belong.'" Gina Corpuz recalled how her father and several other farmhands were assaulted by Island men throwing rocks at them as they were sleeping. "He said they would be so frightened that they would hide under their bunk beds," Corpuz said.

Many, however, continued to work on the strawberry farms. By 1942, when the Japanese Americans were exiled, Island Filipinos had enjoyed close friendships with the Nikkei after more than a decade of employment. An intelligence report for the Thirteenth Naval District in early 1942 lists forty Filipino immigrant farmers associated with seventeen Japanese immigrant farms on Bainbridge. Many of the Nikkei entrusted their farms and homes to the Filipinos during the war, thus preserving their ownership.

Although the U.S. had controlled the Philippines since the Spanish-American War in 1898, its emigrants were treated no differently than other Asians when they arrived here. They could not become citizens, nor could they own land. When the Kitamotos gave Narte part of their property (they sold it to him for one dollar), "This was a big deal because few Filipino farmers had land then," said Narte's granddaughter, Angela Berry. Berry's paternal grandmother, Carmen Rerecich Berry, is the daughter of Yugoslavian immigrants to Bainbridge.

During the war, when pickers were scarce, entire Canadian First Nation Coast Salish families traveled to Bainbridge to work. Since federal law severely restricted immigration from the Philippines and the men far outnumbered the women, romance often blossomed between the young farmhands and the Canadian pickers. Corpuz tells how "my mother and father actually met on a berry farm and fell in love between the strawberry rows." By 1949 federal immigration restrictions were eased, and Asuncion "Cion" Narte became the second Island Filipina bride when she emigrated and married Felix Narte.

Rapada has fond memories of the close relationships between Indopino families and the Nikkei farmers. They would get salmon from her Canadian mother's family— "we'd take as much as we wanted"—and share it with "Mamasan Takemoto" and "Mamasan Suyematsu." Berry also remembers her grandfather telling her of his fondness for "Mama-moto"—Shigeko Kitamoto.

In fact, Narte and Kitamoto forged a partnership. Shigeko's husband, Frank, was employed in Seattle at Friedlander's Jewelry—an unusual occupation for an Island Nikkei—and Shigeko ran the berry farm. Before the war, Narte helped with her four young children. As Kodama recalled, Narte was "like part of the family . . . because [he was] the one who bought me ice cream bars at Bainbridge Gardens grocery."

But it was after the war, and especially after the death of her husband in 1967 that Kitamoto and Narte became "more like brother and sister" according to Kodama. Kodama's brother Frank recalled, "After my father passed away, Felix would stop in and make sure my mom was OK. In his and my mother's later years, I'd come to the house and they'd be playing Chinese checkers."

Kitamoto and Narte shared this mutual reliance into their final years. Once, Kodama went over to their mother's house but couldn't find her. Finally she "looked up on the roof," recalled Frank, "and there were these two eighty-year-olds sitting [there] trying to decide what to do with the hole in the roof." In 1995, at eighty-nine years of age, Kitamoto died. Narte, who was ninety, died shortly thereafter.

"I find the cooperation between the Filipino and Japanese communities on Bainbridge Island unique on the West Coast," said Tom Ikeda of Seattle's Densho Project. "And the addition of native people from Canada makes it an even richer story."

The Kitamoto family, opposite top, shared such a close bond with Felix Narte (right) that Narte visited them at Minidoka. His cousin, Elaulio Akino, opposite bottom with Lilly Kitamoto, also befriended the family. Below: Johnnie Cadavas sent the Hayashida family images of their farm to show them how it was faring while they were incarcerated.

The *Review*'s Open Forum column provided another means of communication between the displaced Islanders and other Bainbridge residents. The Woodwards published every letter they received, as long as it was signed and not libelous.

Three letters ran on April 2, 1942, the first edition after the Islanders left. One from Ichiro Nagatani, a 1933 BHS graduate and leader of the Bainbridge Island chapter of the Japanese American Citizens League, expressed gratitude to the *Review* and the Island. In the letter, Nagatani vowed never to "give you cause to lose that faith in us."

The other two letters illustrate outspoken divisions on Bainbridge. Mrs. Luke Halvorsen of Rolling Bay congratulated the *Review* on its "excellent" editorial stand on the evacuation which, "I believe, well expressed the attitude of the majority of Islanders." J. J. McRee of Port Blakely disagreed and admonished the *Review* for questioning the government's actions, adding bluntly, "The opinions expressed in your rather puerile editorials regarding the evacuation . . . is [sic] quite beyond my comprehension. . . . Please cancel my subscription to your paper as of this week's issue."

In a creative response, Orville Robertson of Battle Point enclosed payment for a new subscription to replace McRee's cancelled one, saying, "May your excellent newspaper gain two new subscribers for each one lost in this way."

Because of their opposition to the incarceration of resident Nikkei, Walt and Milly endured some economic losses. A few businesses pulled their advertising, the lifeblood of any newspaper. Several other readers cancelled their subscriptions. Milly remembered in a 1983 interview for *Visible Target* that "we had some cancellations, more threats than actual." She acknowledged some loss of advertising revenue, but said, "It couldn't have been very much or I would have been aware since I did all the bookkeeping." When the local drugstore called to request more papers to sell over the counter, the couple realized some of the cancelled readers "wouldn't give us the privilege of having their names on our subscription list, but they kept reading" the *Review* because "they had to have the paper to know what was going on."

Throughout the war, and especially as it was ending, Islanders used the Open Forum to talk to each other about the exile and incarceration of their neighbors.

Many Islanders were involved in the war effort. Here, Mamaru Shibukawa (right) visited Islanders at Minidoka while on leave. The Open Forum provided a place for Islanders at home, in the military, and in the camps to keep in contact with each other. Art Koura, opposite above with wife, Florence, often described what was happening to him and fellow Island soldiers in his submissions, opposite bottom.

Escaping the Camps Through Work, College Releases

Even before all West Coast Nikkei had been rounded up and transported to concentration camps, the process that would enable their release was beginning.

In extensive investigations, the FBI and the Justice Department had determined that only a very few of those incarcerated posed any risk, and that assessment was finally heeded. Release was encouraged for a number of other reasons: incarceration was costly, the war effort needed all citizens' participation, and it seemed pointless to continue to interrupt the education of promising students.

Although they were not permitted to return to their homes, inmates were allowed to leave the camps in early summer 1942 to assist in agricultural harvesting. Walt and Milly joined other Islanders, including baseball coach "Pop" Miller, in writing letters vouching for the character of young men who were eager to participate in temporary work release.

Excluded from military service at the time, healthy, strong Nisei were recruited to "save" the crops abandoned by conscripted farmers. The June 18 edition of the *Review* reported, "Barred by circumstances from harvesting their own strawberry crops . . . five Japanese American Islanders left [Manzanar] last week to aid in gathering Idaho's sugar beet crop." By October 1942 there were ten thousand Nisei on seasonal leave, and they were credited with rescuing the sugar beet crop, essential to the war effort, in several western states. Throughout the time of their incarceration, young Islanders, glad to escape the barbed wire and boredom of camp, helped harvest other crops in Idaho and Montana such as potatoes.

While work release was possible, certain conditions applied. Government officials were required to pledge in writing that labor was needed; the workers' safety had to be guaranteed; employers were required to furnish transportation and pay the prevailing wage; and the inmates could not compete with available local labor. In addition, inmates were only allowed to work east of the West Coast military exclusion zones.

From the beginning, the laborers were efficient and pleasant, and they soon were in high demand. By November, the *Review* reported, "The last of the Island's 37 volunteer sugar beet furlough workers returned. . . ." The article continued, "Stepping off the bus were Peter Ohtaki, Winslow, from Idaho Falls, and Harry Yamashita, Winslow, from Sugar City. Weary from their train ride the boys were nevertheless glad to see their parents and friends again. When asked how the work was, Pete Ohtaki replied, 'Oh, it was O.K.'"

The workers, who had left Manzanar for Idaho in September, were glad to have had the opportunity to leave the camp. "Their

general opinion was that they found Idaho to be quite a nice place, they had their enjoyment, and the freedom was worth the hard work," the *Review* reported.

The government also recognized that without educational releases some 3,500 students would be prohibited from continuing their education at colleges and universities. This would result in a significant loss to the nation, as well as to the Nikkei community. No federal money was provided to support these students, and most parents had little savings to contribute, but several groups, notably the Quaker's American Friends Service Committee, provided scholarships. Not every campus was welcoming, and some students encountered discrimination and overt confrontations. But eventually about 4,300 students entered schools from the camps, leaving a lasting impact on Japanese American society as students joined the ranks of working professionals across the country.

Another option was to go on "indefinite leave" to another city. Most exiled Islanders taking advantage of this option settled in Chicago and other areas of the Midwest. Young Nisei found work as domestic help, loggers, clerical workers, and auto mechanics. Many Islanders back home received a form letter from the War Relocation Authority, the civilian agency assigned control of the camps in June 1942, informing them that their names had been "submitted in connection with an application to leave a relocation center of this Authority for employment, education, or residence elsewhere." Many Islanders gladly sent off positive recommendations for young people they had known most of their lives, evaluating the "extent of Americanization" of individuals who had known no other country.

As conditions in the camps deteriorated and outside demands for labor increased, more and more young people moved away. Toward the end of the war, the inmate population was mostly composed of elderly people and mothers with young children. With so many younger camp residents in the military or now living and working in locations across America, a de facto migration was taking place. In yet another way, the people who had been removed from their homes were being pushed into new environments. It was one more factor that would make the return of so many Island Japanese surprising.

Advertisements for jobs that would allow detainees to leave the camps were common in the Manzanar Free Press *as well as other camp journals such as the* Minidoka Irrigator, *opposite. Below: Bruce Nakao (right), son of Islanders Sam and Kay Nakao, played with Louis and Louise Dewey at their Idaho farm, where Sam had come from Minidoka to work.*

One typical wartime letter came from Harry M. Myers in 1943, who did not reside on the Island at that time, but rather in Bremerton:

> Your editorial . . . of the Japanese boys who returned to visit the Island is one of the most inspiring things I've read and I'm proud of you. Nothing less than what you say is "American."
>
> It is regrettable that The Review does not have a hundred thousand circulation as have some papers which express the un-American opposite of your sentiments. Long may you wave.

With the Winslow Shipyard employing thousands of workers, above, and with the nearby naval bases, much of life on the Island during the war centered around social events held at places such as the Navy Housing Project, opposite top. Opposite bottom: An editorial in the Review lambasting Lambert Schuyler for a recent anti-Japanese letter in the Open Forum was evidence of the debate on the Island.

For the most part, the Open Forum carried letters of support for the exiles and letters sharing news with other Islanders. As the war began to wind down in 1944 and the release of the Nikkei seemed imminent, however, Bainbridge Island experienced a little of the rabid racism so evident in communities all along the West Coast.

It began in February with a lengthy letter from Lambert Schuyler of Winslow, a relative newcomer to Bainbridge who hoped to prevent the exiles from returning to the Island. The letter carried this unusual parenthetical preface: "Editor's Note—Views expressed in this letter are not those of The Review. For comment, see editorial column." The letter began,

Bainbridge Islanders are perhaps naturally friendly toward the Japs. We knew them as neighbors, as the smiling and inscrutable operators of truck farms and grocery stores . . . [a]nd as fellow Americans even though they may have been monkey-jawed and yellow-skinned.

PSEUDO-INTELLIGENCE

● Exchanging personal bias for intelligence—cleverly, but we think deliberately—Mr. Lambert Schuyler gives us a diatribe on our Japanese-Americans. We publish it in "The Open Forum" this week because, unlike a few other sneers at the nisei which we've received, it was signed by the writer.

Mr. Schuyler defeats himself, we think, when he blandly claims to speak "intelligently, if to be intelligent is to be self-interested." Webster places no such connotation on "intelligence." He says it is the "product of active intellect."

We don't think it takes any particularly active intellect to refuse to differentiate between a dogma-trained, culture-ridden native of Japan and a free-born, liberty-loving American citizen who happens to have ancestry from the Orient. That blind refusal is clearly indicated by Mr. Schuyler and we think his intelligence takes a sharp nose-dive when he deliberately confuses a Tokyo Jap's torture of American prisoners with the Americans of Japanese descent who once lived here as citizens. He commits a common fault of calling them all "Japs."

An intelligent man doesn't argue with invectives—unless he is driven by personal bias. Yet Mr. Schuyler prefers to call our evacuated friends "monkey-jawed." Well, we won't risk libel by attempting to describe Mr. Schuyler's undoubtedly pretty countenance, but we know our own white-skinned phizz would never win a beauty contest. We've got flop ears and a bulbous beak.

Mr. Schuyler comes closest to being actually intelligent when he describes the unhappy lot which Japanese-Americans face after this war is over. Because there are people like Mr. Schuyler, apparently they will be despised and hated by some —regardless of what sacrifices, even unto death, they may make for their America.

But where else would Mr. Schuyler have them happier—if he cares at all for their happiness? Japan, perhaps? Would Mr. Schuyler please exercise his intelligence a bit and imagine the treatment which would be afforded American citizens—some of whom will be wearing veteran insignias of the United States Army—in Japan? Couldn't it be even worse than the hatred which Mr. Schuyler plans for them here?

Of course, it would only be a blind man who could not see that our white American boys, who are so bravely and savagely fighting the despicable "Jap" in the Pacific, will come back home with hatred in their hearts for anything that faintly resembles the enemy. God will forgive them that very natural reaction, and the rest of us will, too. But while those have to solve their awful post-war race and color problems—to blindly shout, in self-serving bias, that "We don't want any Japs back here ever."

...set heroes of ours are adjust...n that there are some perfect...tens here, it should be our job [the job of every civilian-citi-... period—not to make it infin... hatred...

...use for argument, Mr. Schuy-...to give insult to the ni-... own America. Of course, the ...y of the Japanese-Americans ...chuyler are volunteers; not ...rgument—let us say they are ... writing in the comfort of his ...the holocaust those boys are ...patriotic because they were

..."Il the white American boys being drafted? It leaves them ...riotism and loyalty but merely ...Mr. Schuyler's argument is to ...asion. We hope Mr. Schuyler ...and mothers won't like him if ...the color line.

...essence of Mr. Schuyler's "in-...line. But if we are to deprive ...s and to despise them and hate ... ere to be the objects of scorn ... laying ourselves rather wide ...ter of safeguarding the rights ...sing, in its whimsical way, the ...denly decide tonight that all ... e moved from their homes and ... ere that Mr. Schuyler's name is

...many months stood up for the ...But basically, it makes no dif-...they are Japanese-Americans ...mericans, red-headed Ameri-...They are Americans and, as ...ghts which The Review always

...ent in that stand. We do not ...d of intelligence America must ...

* * * * *

Schuyler suggested an amendment to the Constitution, noting that "it was our ancestors, men who were both white and civilized, who wrote [it]." He then put forth an intricate argument that involved Japan's "barbaric treatment of our men on Bataan" and "the curse which has been laid upon" the Japanese race. "They are unassimilable [sic] as well as despised," he declared, and could be never trusted again. He closed with, "No amount of star-spangled valor on the part of conscripted Japs will change our minds."

Walt, in the editorial response, began by telling readers the *Review* published Schuyler's "diatribe on our Japanese-Americans" because "unlike a few other sneers at the nisei which we've received, it was signed by the writer." Including a bit of humor at his own expense, Walt then countered some of Schuyler's points:

[W]e think his intelligence takes a sharp nose-dive when he deliberately confuses a Tokyo Jap's torture of American prisoners with the Americans of Japanese descent who once lived here as citizens. He commits a common fault of calling them all "Japs."

An intelligent man doesn't argue with invectives—unless he is driven by personal bias. Yet Mr. Schuyler prefers to call our evacuated friends "monkey-jawed." Well, we won't risk libel by attempting to describe Mr.

Nisei Become Military Heroes

Bainbridge Island Nisei were eager to prove their loyalty. In 1941, Walt Woodward had told them only their sacrifice on the battlefield would convince most Americans of their patriotism. His instincts were right. Japanese American soldiers fought valiantly on both fronts and, as time passed, attitudes toward Nikkei changed.

Although the decision to accept Nisei was initially left to individual draft boards, by September 1942 all draft-eligible Nisei were reclassified IV-F (unfit for the military) or IV-C (enemy aliens). It wasn't until 1944 that Nisei could again join the armed services.

Mo Nakata and Kiyotaka "Kiyo" Nagatani were inducted into the army in January 1942, joining four other Island Nisei. Nagatani told the *Review* that military service "gives us an opportunity to really prove we are American citizens and not just talk about it." Nakata's spirited comment was, "I'll give Uncle Sam all I've got."

Nakata's good friend Nob Koura had a different experience. He was turned away from the Air Force recruiter's office in Seattle because he was of Japanese descent. Koura protested, saying, "I am a citizen." The recruiter said, "Not a chance." Koura remembered in 1983, "It was a long walk from that table back out the door. I felt ashamed of myself for being turned down." Koura was eventually drafted.

Sixteen Islanders served in the 442nd, an all-Nisei unit, and six of them were wounded. As one of the war's most decorated units, the 442nd also suffered the highest combat casualty rate of any American fighting unit. The 442nd earned seven Presidential Unit Citations and more than eighteen thousand individual decorations, including twenty Medals of Honor and thirty-four Distinguished Service Crosses.

The 442nd was formed mainly because of the loyalty and valor of another all-Nisei unit. Denying false reports of Nikkei espionage used to justify FDR's order to "lock up [resident Japanese] in concentration camps," Hawaiian Commander Lieutenant General Delos Emmons successfully lobbied against the dissolution of Hawaii's 100th Infantry Battalion. By September 1943 the 100th Battalion was in North Africa and Italy. In less than a year it was joined by the 442nd, and the units saw fierce fighting in Italy and France. Eventually its 522nd Field Artillery Battalion helped liberate the survivors of the notorious death camp at Dachau, Germany.

President Harry S. Truman noted the larger implications of Japanese Americans' remarkable service for their country. "You fought not only the enemy but you fought prejudice—and you won," Truman said, standing in a steady drizzle on the White House lawn in July 1946. "Keep up that fight and we will continue to win—to make this great Republic stand for what the Constitution says it stands for."

The courage of the 442nd is well documented by war correspondents. But another group of some six thousand Nisei men and women fought just as valiantly in the Pacific, but without the public recognition they deserved until very recently.

The Military Intelligence Service (MIS) covertly recruited Nisei from behind barbed wire. The very attributes officials had used so effectively to malign the Nikkei—expertise in the Japanese language and familiarity with the cultural traditions of Japan—were just what was needed to wage war effectively in the Pacific.

One of the best-kept secrets of the war, the MIS proved indispensable, serving in all campaigns and on every front in the Pacific and into China, India, Burma, and even Europe. MIS linguists were part of every landing in the long campaign through the Pacific Islands. They interrogated prisoners and persuaded enemy soldiers to surrender. Their translations of enemy documents allowed Allied commanders to anticipate enemy action and strength, and to attack with surprise. General Douglas MacArthur declared that because of the MIS, "never in military history did an army know so much about the enemy prior to actual engagement."

Major General Frank Merrill of Merrill's Marauders ordered his troops to protect the MIS with their lives. "I couldn't have gotten along without them," he said.

The MIS translation of the Imperial Navy's Order of Battle retrieved on Guadalcanal provided a complete list of every Japanese naval air squadron and air station with their call signs and code names, as well as similar information for every transport and warship in the fleet. The MIS translated the Japanese naval battle plans for the Philippines, Midway, and the Marianas, resulting in such devastating losses for the Imperial Navy that it no longer threatened the Allied advance. After the surrender, the MIS identified war criminals, translated at the war crimes trials, and became an important part of the occupation and reconstruction of Japan.

Paul Ohtaki was one of sixteen Islanders to qualify for the MIS. As part of a twenty-four-man language team, he was assigned to a prisoner of war camp in the Philippines. His team interrogated and processed thousands of Japanese prisoners, both military and civilian. He finished his tour at general headquarters in Tokyo.

Major General Charles Willoughby, chief of intelligence for MacArthur, praised the interpreters' work, saying, "The Nisei shortened the Pacific war by two years and saved possibly a million American lives."

Major General Clayton Bissell, chief of the Military Intelligence Division of the War Department, advised, "If you Japanese Americans are ever questioned as to your loyalty, don't even bother to reply. . . . Your gallant deeds under fire will speak so loudly that you need not answer."

Some thirty-three thousand Nisei were in the military during World War II, including sixty-six men and two women from Bainbridge Island. One of those, Toshio "Paul" Sakai, spoke of their overriding motivation. "There's a point where we actually put our life on the line," Sakai said. "That's what it was. So that we can be part of this society and be an American."

Even though their families were incarcerated, many Island Nisei fought valiantly for their country during the war. Mo Nakata earned both a Bronze Star and a Purple Heart, opposite, during his service in the 442nd, while the Review's *former janitor and camp reporter, Paul Ohtaki, below, served in the Military Intelligence Service.*

Schuyler's undoubtedly pretty countenance, but we know our own white-skinned phizz would never win a beauty contest. We've got flop ears and a bulbous beak.

Supposing, in its whimsical way, the federal authorities should suddenly decide tonight that all people named Schuyler should be moved from their homes and bundled back to the interior, there to be objects of scorn by the rest of us. Does it matter that Mr. Schuyler's name is not Yamamoto?

The Review has for many, many months stood up for the Japanese-Americans, it is true. But basically, it makes no difference to The Review whether they are Japanese-Americans, German-Americans, Italian-Americans, red-headed Americans or Schuyler-Americans. They are Americans and, as such, are guaranteed certain rights which The Review will always defend.

As dramatic as this exchange was, nothing much came of it. It wasn't until autumn that things really began to heat up—Schuyler organized the Live and Let Live Legion to prevent Island Japanese from returning to their homes. Its first meeting was advertised in postcard notices sent to Islanders. The topic was the "Jap problem." Milly, accompanied by her young daughter, covered the gathering for the *Review*. As Milly recalled in 1983, some two hundred people listened as Schuyler proposed sending all Japanese Americans, along with all "Jap-lovers, which I'm sure included the Woodwards, to some island in the Pacific where they could be by themselves."

Milly's report detailed the events of the evening, including the distribution of posters reading "Banish Japs from this coast forever. Remember Pearl Harbor League." Schuyler castigated the *Review* for its editorial stand and unsuccessfully tried to prepare a list of those willing to cancel their subscriptions. He also urged people to write letters "indicating that The Review does not represent the majority sentiment on the Island."

The meeting was heated at times. One person, at least, was heckled while trying to defend the return of Island Nikkei. Others wanted to know the purpose of the meeting, with one attendee asking, "Do we want the Japs back? . . . Or is this a personal feud between Mr. Schuyler and Mr. Woodward?" Another person "was well applauded" for calling the segregation of Native Americans on reservations a precedent that justified the Nikkei incarceration.

COMMITTEE NAMED TO OPPOSE JAPANESE RETURN; 200 ATTEND MEETING

Major M. J. Hopkins, a transplanted Brit who was scoutmaster for a troop that before the war had included several Nisei Boy Scouts, acknowledged that the question of their return was personally "unpleasant." The *Review* continued, "He said, however, that he did not want them again as neighbors." Schuyler suggested, "Let's put down Woodward as our asset [Number] One. He keeps us stirred up."

Milly and Walt's editorial in response may have surprised a few Islanders when it praised the "free American citizens [who] decided to hold a meeting and speak their minds in free assembly." The couple encouraged Islanders to continue the conversation, saying, "Our readers always have been welcome to use our 'Open Forum' column to discuss controversial issues, for only by discussion and thought can America solve its many postwar problems."

In the next few weeks, readers took full advantage of their offer. Opinions both pro and con were aired as Bainbridge Islanders talked with each other in a stream of letters to the editor:

Mildred E. Cumle concluded her lengthy letter with, "If we are to have peace and harmony we must respect the rights of all men. Let's start by treating our Japanese neighbors as human beings and forget ancestors. Keep up the fight for right, Mr. and Mrs. Editor."

Local realtor Russell Munro offered to help Island Nikkei dispose "of their Island farms and other properties so they, too, could reestablish elsewhere. . . . [T]he sooner new interests purchase . . . [Island Japanese land] the better it will be for all concerned."

Mrs. W. M. Williams congratulated Milly "on the very fair account of a meeting which so scurillously [sic] attacked you and your newspaper."

Katherine Warner wrote, "I was raised with Japanese neighbors and attended school with them for twelve years. I saw them learn all they could from us . . . and yet I can truthfully say I . . . [have never] learned one single thing from a Jap! . . . I, like Major Hopkins, do not want them as my neighbors!"

Lottie Jane Logg declared, "I think the question is not shall the return of the Jap be allowed, but can we dictate to any American citizen where they shall live? If we can so dictate, no doubt many of us will get busy and have some of our neighbors moved, and we had all better get uneasy about our own permanency."

At the initial meeting of Lambert Schuyler's Live and Let Live Legion to oppose the return of the displaced Islanders, some two hundred residents of the Island attended. Milly, opposite, who covered the meeting, and Walt responded to it in an editorial, below. In it, they supported the group's right to free speech while decrying its message. Subsequent meetings were not as well attended.

THE ANTI-JAPANESE SPEAK

● Some 200 of the 7,000 people on this Island attended a meeting last week which discussed action to prevent the return here of those of Japanese ancestry whom the Army evacuated more than two years ago.

The Review fails to see that numbers are important in the basic consideration of this problem. The point is that some free American citizens decided to hold a meeting and speak their minds in free assembly. This, The Review thinks, is good.

If those in charge of the next meeting will take the trouble to let The Review know about it, this newspaper will give the meeting ample advance notice. It is unfortunate that The Review wasn't asked to provide publicity on the first meeting, for more free Americans might have joined in the discussion.

The Review realizes only too well that the Island (like many other West Coast communities) must face up to a serious problem in the impending return to this section of evacuees. Our readers always have been welcome to use our "Open Forum" column to discuss controversial issues, for only by discussion and thought can America solve its many postwar problems. Feeling this way, The Review certainly welcomes any public meetings to thrash things out.

The Review, of course, cannot subscribe to some of the extreme ideas presented at last week's meeting. For years now, we have stood by one point and one point only. We still say, despite the gathering held last week, that the majority of Islanders believe with us in that point, namely that citizenship rights guaranteed in our Constitution must not be tossed aside because of a war hysteria.

We believe the majority of the Island agrees with us that it is a dangerous thing for us to decide suddenly that we will deprive one group of citizens of their inherent rights under the Constitution. We believe we speak the majority opinion that such a destruction of citizenship for one group could lead easily to similar loss of rights for another and then another segment of our citizenry. This is the awful thing that happened in fascist Italy and nazi Germany. We are sure that America wants none of this.

Certainly, The Review admires the exercise of free speech last week as guaranteed by our Constitution. We hope those who disagree with us similarly respect our use of the right of a free press. In this connection we regret to note that one person who had the interest and courage to speak out in opposition to the majority at last week's meeting was heckled and had his patriotism questioned.

Surely that is not the way to arrive at a sensible solution to this problem. We are very near, indeed, to a totalitarian situation in this nation if those who disagree with us must be called unpatriotic.

We hope that those who would bar the return of our evacuee citizens will remember at their next free American assembly that they meet under the protection of the greatest governmental document ever written—the Constitution of the United States.

Let them be guided less by hysteria and blind, war-inflamed viewpoints. Let them, instead, turn to logic. Above all, let them take care that they do not destroy the very guarantee which gives them, as American citizens, the right to free speech and free assembly.

• • • • •

The Japs Must Not Come Back!

by Lambert Schuyler

25 cents

A second meeting of the Live and Let Live Legion garnered a meager forty in attendance, including six children and a somber Walt Woodward, who listened as speaker after speaker attacked him and the *Review.* His lone defender, Louise Gregg, was dismissed as a communist. As the master of ceremonies and principal speaker, Lambert Schuyler distributed cards reading, "We live in our country—let the Japs live in theirs!" He declared that when the authors of the Declaration of Independence "wrote that 'all men are created equal,' they meant all white men are created equal." Mostly, he attacked the editor, accusing him of a smear campaign. "We're not trying to cause [trouble]," Schuyler said. "It's only in Woodward's paper that we're sowing seeds of hatred and are un-American."

Some of the most overtly racist public comments by Islanders were recorded at that meeting. Their words were duly reported in full in the *Review.* After reading them, though, the Island lost whatever interest it had in the Live and Let Live Legion. As Walt recalled in a 1983 interview, "Bainbridge Island wanted to know what was going on, and when it found out, it had nothing to do with running the Japanese off the Island."

As the reports of the two anti-Japanese meetings became known beyond the Island, the *Review* received letters of support, many from Island servicemen—both Nisei and Caucasian—and others from Seattle, Oregon, California, and Florida.

But, while Milly and Walt appreciated these, they were particularly concerned by a personal letter from Sa Koura Nakata, who offered to stop the reports from Minidoka if that might help quell some of the public criticism of her employers. While the rumblings of anti-Japanese talk on Bainbridge had grown to an energetic, if brief, shout, Nakata had been receiving unsolicited and unwelcome correspondence in Minidoka. Walt responded,

> You said you didn't know whether The Review wants you to continue sending the news articles. H---, yes! A guy named Schuyler doesn't own The Review; not yet, anyway. When you're fired, we'll let you know in plenty of time.

In a second letter, Walt, as usual, started with a light comment and closed on a serious note.

No, let's *not* let the column drop.

You, particularly, have done extremely well with it. . . . I don't recall ever having given it any close scrutiny, but I would say that your nose for news is a good one.

About letting the column drop temporarily, it's like this. The Review has stuck its neck out good and proper for you people not because you are "you people" but because you are Americans and, temporarily, have lost the citizenship right this nation guarantees to every citizen. The news from [Minidoka], despite the fact that this sounds a bit like a speech, is a torch held high in the name of good American citizenship. Its flame reminds the people of Bainbridge Island and all who care to read The Review that some of our neighbors—our fellow citizens—are living elsewhere temporarily. It is a torch which has burned steadily since a very bad day in December, 1941. Don't let it's [sic] light go out—even temporarily.

Racist signs and graffiti, opposite top, were common on the West Coast. On the Island, Lambert Schuyler spread his dislike for both the Nikkei and the Woodwards in letters to the Open Forum and in a book, opposite bottom, but he was in the minority. Below: In a letter to their camp reporter, Sa Koura Nakata, Walt urged her to keep up with her articles for the Review despite the heated debate back home.

As 1945 began, the *Bainbridge Review* was full of news of Islanders in uniform. It ran regular features such as "Footsteps to Freedom" and "They've Gone to War," and it continued its Open Forum, often with letters such as this from Technical Sergeant Rodney Waldron: "I'll fight Tojo's Nips from here to breakfast, but our own Japanese Americans deserve the same consideration as other American-born [citizens]. . . . The Japanese were part of the scheme of things before I left, and I for one, want them back."

As the end of the war seemed near, it appeared the incarcerated Islanders would soon be freed and allowed to return to the home they had so hurriedly left three long years before. It also seemed likely that Island Nikkei would encounter more welcomes than barriers.

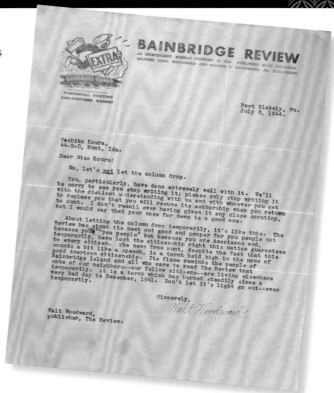

Surrounded by their old friends and neighbors from Bainbridge Island, Milly and Walt Woodward (center) were recognized by the surviving Manzanar alumni at the second Manzanar Reunion in 1987. At the event, the Woodwards were given an award recognizing them as "Defenders of the Constitution" and presented with an artistic interpretation of the camp by one of the attendees.

4

A HOMECOMING
FOR SOME

nose subversion and sabotage. None of the scare stories circulated during the period were ever substantiated. Nevertheless, public figures and influential groups called out insistently for the removal of all Japanese Americans from the coast.

On February 19, 1942, President Franklin D. Roosevelt responded by signing Executive Order 9066. This authorized the Army to remove civilians from the country which it deemed necessary.

Two weeks later, Lieutenant General John of the Western Defense Command, de West Coast off limits to all persons of Ja In a series of military orders Japanese instructed to dispose of their homes, nesses, and to report to evacuation ce 110,000 people were affected, about t native born Americans.

To house these evacuees, ten internment camps in remote desert areas of the inland West. Th were originally intended as temporary housing uees who would be resettled in non-restricted two years later, most Japanese Americans camp, and these camps continued to operate until after the end of World War II.

The bitter Ameri nounc

Fifteen months before the army allowed the Nikkei to return to the West Coast, Mo "Pork Chops" Nakata and Art Koura came home for a visit. A *Review* editorial explained, "Art and 'Pork Chops,' as 'American' a pair as ever trod the corridors of Bainbridge High School, were permitted to visit here because they wear the uniforms of the United States Army. Uncle Sam, who soon may ask them to die for him, couldn't very well tell them they couldn't come home on furlough." Although soldiers visited the Island, the rest of the Nikkei remained incarcerated in the camps until nearly the end of the war.

EDISON UNO
CIVIL RIGHTS AWARD
NATIONAL JACL CONVENTION
CHICAGO   7-21-86

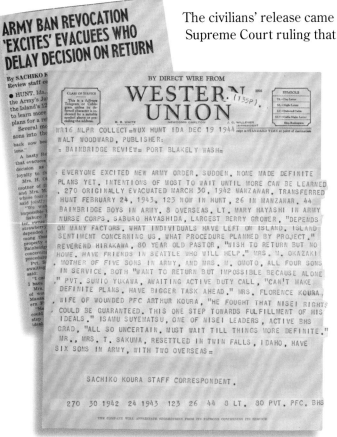

ARMY BAN REVOCATION 'EXCITES' EVACUEES WHO DELAY DECISION ON RETURN

By SACHIKO K
Review staff corr

● HUNT, Ida.,
the Army's Ja
the Island's 12
to learn more
plans for a re
Several mo
sons into the
back now bec
lone."
A hasty Re
that evacuees
decision as
loyalty to th
Mrs. H. O
mother of fi
and Mrs. M.
whose four
said jointly
"We war
impossible f
Saburo
strawberry
ted, owner
depended o
property"
mong thos
Bainbridge
concerning
procedure
Pvt. S
awaiting
said:
"I ca
I have
Mrs.
of wou
Manzan
ern Fi
"Be
could
step f
ideas

BY DIRECT WIRE FROM

WESTERN UNION

WR16 NLPR COLLECT=WUX HUNT IDA DEC 19 1944
WALT WOODWARD, PUBLISHER:
= BAINBRIDGE REVIEW= PORT BLAKELY WASH=

- EVERYONE EXCITED NEW ARMY ORDER. SUDDEN. NONE MADE DEFINITE PLANS YET. INTENTIONS OF MOST TO WAIT UNTIL MORE CAN BE LEARNED . 270 ORIGINALLY EVACUATED MARCH 30, 1942 MANZANAR, TRANSFERRED HUNT FEBRUARY 24, 1943, 123 NOW IN HUNT, 26 IN MANZANAR. 44 BAINBRIDGE BOYS IN ARMY. 8 OVERSEAS. LT. MARY HAYASHI IN ARMY NURSE CORPS. SABURO HAYASHIDA, LARGEST BERRY GROWER, "DEPENDS ON MANY FACTORS. WHAT INDIVIDUALS HAVE LEFT ON ISLAND. ISLAND SENTIMENT CONCERNING US. WHAT PROCEDURE PLANNED BY PROJECT." REVEREND HIRAKAWA, 80 YEAR OLD PASTOR, "WISH TO RETURN BUT NO HOME. HAVE FRIENDS IN SEATTLE WHO WILL HELP." MRS. M. OKAZAKI . MOTHER OF FIVE SONS IN ARMY, AND MRS. M. OMOTO, ALL FOUR SONS IN SERVICE, BOTH "WANT TO RETURN BUT IMPOSSIBLE BECAUSE ALONE ." PVT. SUMIO YUKAWA, AWAITING ACTIVE DUTY CALL, "CAN'T MAKE DEFINITE PLANS. HAVE BIGGER TASK AHEAD." MRS. FLORENCE KOURA, WIFE OF WOUNDED PFC ARTHUR KOURA, "HE FOUGHT THAT NISEI RIGHTS COULD BE GUARANTEED. THIS ONE STEP TOWARDS FULFILLMENT OF HIS IDEALS." ISAMU SUYEMATSU, ONE OF NISEI LEADERS, ACTIVE BHS GRAD, "ALL SO UNCERTAIN. MUST WAIT TILL THINGS MORE DEFINITE." MR., MRS. T. SAKUMA, RESETTLED IN TWIN FALLS, IDAHO, HAVE SIX SONS IN ARMY, WITH TWO OVERSEAS =

SACHIKO KOURA STAFF CORRESPONDENT.

270 30 1942 24 1943 123 26 44 8 LT. 80 PVT. PFC. BHS

THE COMPANY WILL APPRECIATE SUGGESTIONS FROM ITS PATRONS CONCERNING ITS SERVICE.

The civilians' release came in January 1945. This was, in part, the result of a U.S. Supreme Court ruling that the WRA had no authority to detain a "concededly loyal" American citizen. In November 1944, President Roosevelt remarked, "A good deal of progress has been made in scattering them throughout the country. . . . And it is felt by a great many lawyers that under the Constitution they can't be kept locked up in concentration camps."

After nearly three years of imprisonment, the U.S. government released the incarcerated American citizens and their parents. The mass detention of Nikkei was over. The facilities were decommissioned and all were closed by early 1946.

The incarceration had forced nearly 120,000 people to leave their homes and businesses. The majority of them lost everything they had before the war—estimates run in the hundreds of millions in 1941 dollars. They had nothing to return to. In addition, many communities actively campaigned to keep these former neighbors, these "Japs," from returning.

Barely a month after the ban was lifted in January 1945, Sam Nakao returned to check on his family's land and "prospects on the Island." Now married to the former Kay Sakai and the father of one-year-old Bruce, he had read the reports about the anti-Japanese meetings on Bainbridge. His wife was determined to return, but he needed to talk to some friends to be sure.

Johnny Nakata was also concerned for his wife and three young sons. He came to the Island for a short visit and later contacted the Woodwards, wondering how his family would be received, and if it "would be safe for his boys." Milly said in a 1983 interview, "Walt wrote back to assure him we thought they would be. So they came back and they certainly were received! They run the biggest grocery on Bainbridge Island." Islanders at Minidoka yet to decide about their futures eagerly listened to reports from Nakata and Nakao on what they had learned on their visits.

As the exiles were freed, groups responsible for much of the prewar anti-Japanese racism—the American Legion, the Grange, and the Native Sons of the Golden West—continued to encourage action against the Nikkei. The Hood River, Oregon, post of the American Legion and the Veterans of Foreign Wars in Gardena, California, struck the names of Japanese American soldiers from public honor rolls in 1945. An Arizona barber refused to cut the hair of a decorated, wounded vet because he was Japanese American. In some instances, Nikkei homes were doused with gasoline and set aflame, and guns were fired at some of the returning Americans.

David Beck, leader of Seattle's powerful Teamsters Union, used his group to prevent Japanese Americans from bringing their produce to public markets, while Northwest fruit growers, florists, and produce merchants organized a boycott of Nikkei farms. On Vashon, another Puget Sound island located just south of Bainbridge, three young people were convicted of burning the home of a family incarcerated at Minidoka. The family's insurance had been cancelled when the war began. Although the structure was totally destroyed along with all the family's furnishings and belongings, the local court ordered the youths to pay only nominal restitution.

Public officials like Washington's newly elected governor, Mon C. Wallgren, opposed any return of Nikkei. According to a January 23, 1945, article in the *Seattle Post-Intelligencer*, Wallgren "implied that the public has not been fully informed on the extent of underground Japanese-American collaboration with Japan." As late as April 1945, Senator Warren G. Magnuson was calling for the mass deportation of "any American-born Japanese" who had stated or implied his loyalty to Hirohito. Congressman Henry M. "Scoop" Jackson, who with Magnuson had supported the incarceration, continued to

Although the news of their release, opposite top, excited many of the Island Nikkei, they were cautious about their return. Anti-Japanese sentiment, like the notorious display in G. S. Hantf's Kent, Washington, barber shop, above, was common around the country. Opposite bottom: A telegram from Sa Koura Nakata to Walt describing the Island Nikkei's situation following the news of their release.

work to prevent the return of the Nikkei to his hometown of Everett. In Kent, Washington, G. S. Hantf grinned as the camera caught him proudly pointing to a sign in his barber shop that read, "WE DON'T WANT ANY JAPS BACK HERE—EVER!" Oregon passed a measure strengthening its existing alien land law, a clear message that the Nikkei were unwelcome.

Newspapers, an essential element of earlier anti-Japanese activity, again chimed in. *Time* magazine reported in March 1945 that five hundred residents of a town in Oregon had added their names to a full-page newspaper ad proclaiming: "So Sorry Please. Japs Are Not Wanted in Hood River." Closer to home, Miller Freeman's *Bellevue American* published reports in the spring of 1945 of unsubstantiated rumors about "Jap spy rings" aiding the enemy. Its articles helped publicize community meetings of the Japanese Exclusion League. Like its cousin, the Remember Pearl Harbor League (formed by white farmers in Kent, Renton, Auburn, and surrounding towns

ARTHUR KOURA, WOUNDED IN WAR, RETURNED TO U.S.

By Sachiko Koura

● HUNT, Ida.— ~~~ ry 5.—Pfc.
~~~ ita, wound-
France on
~~~ eturned to
~~~ l ship re-
~~~ m as yet
~~~ rred. Pfc.
serving in

TWO MORE ISLAND NISEI WOUNDED IN FRENCH ACTION

By SACHIKO KOURA
Review Staff Correspondent

● HUNT, Ida.—Thursday, Novem-
ber 23.—Two more Island nisei— ood Cen-
Sergt. Momoichi Nakata and Pvt. ew days'
William Okazaki — have been gradu-
wounded in action in France, this shington
relocation center was advised this d major-
week.

An earlier dispatch last week
said that PFC Arthur Koura, Man- Blakely,
zanita, was the first Island nisei the lo-
to be wounded. said to

Sergeant Nakata, Winslow, not-
ed as a basketball player at Bain- as one
bridge High School, received slight week.
wounds October 28, the same day bridge
on which Private Koura was hurt.
The sergeant's parents reside in
the relocation center at Manzanar, hers
Calif. Sergeant Nakata was draft- two
ed in February, 1942. o be

Private Okazaki, Winslow, vol- on.
unteered from Hunt. His mother
resides here. Like Sergeant Nakata, he went overseas last May.

Tochio Suyematsu, Port Madison, went to Pocatello, Ida., last
week for his pre-induction physical
examination. Accompanying him
was Tony Koura, Manzanita, who
was inducted and who is in the
Army Enlisted Reserve Corps.

Kenneth Nakata, Winslow, a visitor here for a few days, left for
Chicago.

south of Seattle), this group attracted five hundred people to a meeting by asking, "Do you want Japs for your neighbors again?" Unlike Bainbridge's anti-Japanese Live and Let Live Legion, the league's influence did not die after its first few meetings.

In this atmosphere of negative public opinion, it is a rare person who has the courage to speak against the crowd, to be the lone voice raised against accepted community goals, especially those supported by elected officials and the media. In Bellevue and Everett and other nearby communities, the accepted community goal was to prevent the Nikkei's return. In each of those communities there were some who welcomed the Japanese Americans back, but their voices were drowned out.

In 1992, fifty years after her exile as a teenager, one Bellevue woman told a local reporter, "For most, there was nothing to come back to. . . . There still is a subtle, residual hostility [in Bellevue]. Although we have friends, there still are some people who would prefer if we did not return."

It was different for the Bainbridge Island exiles. "When the ban was lifted I was in Chicago," recalled Jerry Nakata in 2002. "I hopped a plane and came right home. That's what Bainbridge meant to me." Unlike many communities, Bainbridge was welcoming aside from a few, mostly reticent, detractors. "My closest friend, Reese Moran, met me at the ferry dock," he said. "I remember the good things that the Caucasians did for me and my family. I [am] very grateful for that."

In communities where the principal public voice—often the newspaper—was opposed to the return of the Nikkei, few returned. The Hearst chain and the *Sacramento Bee* did much to encourage racism in their readers. In contrast, as Bainbridge Island's public voice, the *Review* paved the way for the exiles' return and inspired its readers to act on their good intentions.

Milly and Walt reported the news—all the news—and let the community form its own judgements. Islanders not only knew what Lambert Schuyler and M. J. Hopkins were saying, but how Private Art Koura and Private William Okazaki were doing while recuperating from wounds they sustained while fighting with the 442nd. The couple also gave the Island a forum for discussion—the Open Forum—and allowed Islanders to talk to each other through letters to the editor. Thus, Bainbridge Islanders had a platform to express their support of their neighbors, something that was often lacking in other communities.

In that atmosphere on Bainbridge, people were not afraid to speak out against the exclusion. At the same time, those who supported the exclusion were ultimately overshadowed, tempering their public comments because the tide had turned so resoundingly toward support for the Nikkei. Elinor Yost was one Islander willing to go on the record. In 1960, she told Walt and Milly's second daughter, "You know, not everyone on the Island agreed with your father." In 1983 Yost explained her reasoning to an interviewer, saying, "It would have taken months to sift through the Japanese population and decide who was a loyal citizen and who was not. It was much more expedient to send all of them to an area where they could be controlled." But she was in the minority and, as the war came to an end, Bainbridge Islanders as a group rejected the racism that flowered in nearby communities.

The dialogue afforded by the *Review* even influenced Walt's thoughts on some issues. Throughout the early years of the exclusion, Walt would often contrast the internment of Issei with the incarceration of Japanese American citizens, pointing out that internment of "enemy aliens" was perfectly legal. Milly, however, never saw it from this perspective. She concurred with Walt that the practice may have been legal but countered that legality didn't necessarily make it right. Over the years, Walt's insistence on this distinction softened somewhat.

In April, the *Review* announced, "Takemotos Return to Island Home," and gave an account of the "first evacuated Japanese family to make a permanent return to the Island." Saichi and Yone Takemoto and five of their six children (one son had married) arrived around evening without the prescribed WRA escort, who visited the next day. The *Review* reported:

> The family arrived to find their former home at Rolling Bay a shambles. Windows were broken and much of the family's personal property, which had been stored at the home, was gone.

TAKEMOTOS RETURN TO ISLAND HOME

Because Milly and Walt, opposite top, reported on the Island Nikkei's life in the camps and military, opposite bottom, the Nikkei remained part of the community, despite their exclusion. Therefore, most eventually returned. Right: The Takemoto family was the first family to permanently return to Bainbridge Island.

> The Rev. Charles P. Milne, pastor of the Winslow Congregational Church, and other Islanders aided the family with emergency donations of bedding and other household necessities after the family spent its first night sleeping under overcoats.

> The Takemoto strawberry farm was filled with weeds. It was doubtful if a crop could be produced before next summer, if then.

Three weeks later, after the Takemotos had reclaimed two acres, twenty members of the American Friends Service Committee, mostly students at the University of Washington, spent a day working on the Takemoto farm. "Despite the rainy weather, an acre of ground

The Ongoing Fight For Legal Vindication

During war, it is hard for anyone to challenge the government, particularly a small group intent on proving its loyalty—and with no political clout. Indeed, few Nikkei challenged their wartime incarceration. Protest must have seemed futile, and government reprisals were swift and unyielding. Two of the Manzanar "rioters" died after soldiers fired on the unarmed crowd. Those who resisted were often sent to the Tule Lake Segregation Center, the only camp under martial law and occupied by the army.

Even so, more than one hundred Japanese Americans deliberately violated orders, hoping to challenge Executive Order 9066 in court on constitutional grounds. Of these, the government selected four cases for prosecution.

Fred Korematsu, a San Francisco welder before the war, had only wanted to stay with his girlfriend when he defied the order to "relocate." Arrested by military police in May 1942, Korematsu was in the county jail when he met Ernest Besig, a young attorney with the American Civil Liberties Union. Korematsu was convicted of violating a military order and confined in the Topaz, Utah, concentration camp, where other inmates shunned him for resisting. Besig appealed the conviction, but in December 1944, the Supreme Court denied the appeal, saying an American citizen could be jailed for defying an order based only on ancestry.

Two other challenges—by University of Washington student Gordon Hirabayashi and Oregon attorney and Army Reserve Second Lieutenant Minoru Yasui—also failed. But one case prevailed. Mitsuye Endo petitioned for a writ of habeas corpus stating that she was a loyal and law-abiding U.S. citizen being unlawfully confined under armed guard against her will. The Supreme Court agreed, declaring that such indefinite detention was illegal. However, the decision was limited and did not comment on the constitutionality of the overall incarceration.

Then, nearly forty years later, two researchers using the Freedom of Information Act unearthed a wartime memo from a Department of Justice lawyer that clearly showed how federal prosecutors in the "Japanese American Cases" had withheld crucial evidence, including military reports stating Japanese Americans posed no serious threat to U.S. security. One of those scholars, Peter Irons of the University of California at San Diego, contacted Korematsu and told him he could ask the courts to correct a "manifest injustice."

"General DeWitt had been told there was no such evidence [that Japanese Americans were disloyal] before he issued the curfew and evacuation orders, and . . . he disregarded what he was told," Irons wrote. "Since the government had this evidence at the time of your trial, it was under an obligation to produce it. By failing to produce it, the court's judgment of guilty . . . was based on error and a fundamental injustice was committed."

Irons also contacted Hirabayashi and Yasui, and all agreed to file petitions in court. Korematsu explained to the media that he was willing to revisit that painful time, "because they can do this again to . . . any American. How safe are we?"

When Walt and Milly heard the news of Irons's discovery, they remembered how they had agonized over wartime events. In a letter to Paul Ohtaki, Walt expressed their delight in the proof "that DeWitt was a liar after all." Walt also told Ohtaki how the news had dredged up old feelings of anger, "[remembering] how hopeless and discouraged we were when . . . along comes DeWitt, in all his might and majesty, charging 'Japanese' with being traitors, etc." He continued, "What could we do? Nothing. We were at war and you don't call a general a liar unless you have a pile of facts. And we didn't have any facts, and no way to get them." The letter concluded with Walt's hope that the legal challenges would be successful: "It's the only way to go. . . . A U.S. Supreme Court reversal would mean a great deal."

Korematsu, Hirabayashi, and Yasui each petitioned to have his criminal conviction overturned. Each was successful. Judge Marilyn Patel of the U.S. District Court in San Francisco overturned Korematsu's conviction in 1983, declaring there had been no military necessity for the orders. DeWitt's views were tainted with racism, she said, and the U.S. government had illegally suppressed, altered, and destroyed evidence critical to the 1944 Supreme Court decision. Some eight hundred people, mostly Japanese Americans, listened in stunned silence and then erupted with applause and tears. One of the attorneys said, "It was the trial they never had."

However, because a lower court cannot overturn a Supreme Court ruling, although the convictions were reversed, the 1944 Supreme Court rulings still stand. The only way a case gets to the Supreme Court is on an appeal of an unsatisfactory ruling. The Nisei defendants had been vindicated, thus they had nothing to appeal. Because the Department of Justice chose not to challenge the reversals, the nation's highest court was never asked to reconsider its 1944 rulings.

Almost twenty years earlier, FBI director J. Edgar Hoover had suggested the possibility of concentration camps to hinder "Red Chinese infiltration." In response, on December 7, 1969, Walt wrote in the *Seattle Times*, "[We] must remember that *Hirabayashi v. United States* . . . still stands as an unreversed decision . . . and thus places in doubt the conceptions which most Americans have of the inviolability of their citizenship rights. . . ."

Arguing that the evacuation of the Japanese Americans twenty-seven years earlier still had relevance, Walt continued, "That evacuation, taken especially in context with the new threat to citizens of Chinese descent, proves that citizenship rights cannot be taken for granted. Those rights—now, as then, and for evermore—must be remembered well, articulated plainly and defended courageously if they are to be valid."

Although the Korematsu, Hirabayashi, and Yasui petitions brought up painful memories for many, including the Woodwards, their victories made the opening of old wounds worthwhile. In a letter to longtime friend Paul Ohtaki, below, Walt and Milly expressed their joy at Professor Irons's discoveries and their wishes for the success of the upcoming trials.

was prepared and planted with strawberry plants," the *Review* reported.

All up and down the Pacific Coast that spring and summer, newly released families returned to vandalized houses and damaged or stolen personal property. Bainbridge families also saw damage, but to a lesser degree. There was vandalism—common whenever a house stands vacant—but it was a result more of petty crime and greed than viciousness. There was at least one racist slogan, "but the boys washed it off," recalled Sa Nakata years later.

In Bellevue only eleven of the more than sixty Nikkei families returned to their former homes, according to David A. Niewert's *Strawberry Days: How Internment Destroyed a Japanese American Community*. In Hood River, Oregon, less than 40 percent of its exiles came back. In California, only one out of every four farmers returned to the land. In contrast, Bainbridge Island saw the return of more than half of those exiled. "They didn't come back as strangers. We already knew that so-and-so had married so-and-so and had a baby boy, and we were looking forward to meeting the new baby," Walt recalled.

Many of the farms the Island Nikkei had been forced to leave were still there for them because a neighbor had made sure the taxes were paid. "They took care of things for us. We even got our horse back!" recalled Paul Sakai in 1975. Classmates welcomed returning friends, eager to get caught up. Neighbors assisted returning neighbors, bringing food and blankets and helping to clean up where there was damage.

"People came back without incident," Walt explained in a 1983 interview. "Neither were they welcomed with a brass band, nor were they welcomed with barn burnings. Nothing. They just came back."

That's not to say their return was always easy. One family found it simpler to sell its home and farm to its caretaker than risk a perhaps violent confrontation over the exorbitant price he was attempting to extort for his labor and crops during the war. Zenhichi Harui and his family were devastated to see the dilapidated condition of Bainbridge Gardens, which had been their business and a renowned garden and nursery. According to his son, Junkoh, Zenhichi's heart was broken, and he never found the strength to rebuild. It wasn't until thirty years later that Junkoh and his wife, Chris, began the process of returning the garden to its former glory. Bainbridge Gardens today is cherished by Islanders who visit—not always with a purchase in mind—seeking its peace and beauty.

When renovating, Harui set aside a portion of the property as a memorial to his parents, centered on his father's delightful pear tree, whose dual trunks were formed into the shape of a pear as the tree was growing. Crossing a small bridge, visitors encounter a forest of Japanese red pines. Hastily tossed aside in 1942 as the family scrambled

The Harui family, owners of Bainbridge Gardens, returned to the Island to find their property in shambles. Thirty years later, Junkoh Harui, shown here with his father's prized pear tree, returned the gardens to their former beauty. Opposite (clockwise from top): Yoshihiro Harui, Junkoh Harui, Zenji Shibayama, Norio Harui, and an unidentified boy (in dark shirt) at Bainbridge Gardens in its prewar heyday.

For young people such as Yaeko Sakai, whose 1945–46 Student Association card is pictured opposite, going to school and joining teams and clubs made the transition back easier. By the time the youngest, like Frank Kitamoto, opposite top (right), were teenagers their lives were not much different than any other kids'. Above: Ken Nakata picks strawberries on the farm his family once had to abandon.

to leave, the small trees—started from seeds brought from Japan—soon burst from their pots and took root. They now tower above a meandering salmon stream.

By the end of July 1945, Shigeko and Frank Kitamoto and their children were back in their Fletcher Bay home. Also back home in Winslow were Yosuke and Ume Moji, an older, childless couple whose beautiful white Samoyed, unable to accompany them in 1942, had died after refusing to eat.

Some who wanted to return, unfortunately, could not. Kusunosuke Kino and his family lost their prosperous strawberry farm when the taxes went unpaid. They settled in Idaho. Two widows, Masu Okazaki and Masa Omoto, who together had nine sons in the MIS and 442nd, told *Review* reporter Sa Koura Nakata at Minidoka, "We want to return, but it is impossible because we are alone." And farmers who could only lease land before the war had no property to return to.

Others chose to settle elsewhere. Saburo and Fumiko Hayashida, co-owners of the Island's largest berry farm, decided not to return to the hard life of farming. Saburo Hayashida found work at Boeing and the family moved to Seattle. The large Sakuma family, who had eight sons and two daughters, discovered the farming was better in the rich Skagit River Valley. Those who were teenagers in 1942 were now young adults and many of them settled elsewhere when they married or found employment—in areas such as Utah, Minnesota, Illinois, and the eastern Washington town of Moses Lake.

If there is any silver lining to the dark cloud of the exclusion, it is that it broadened the horizons of young Japanese Americans who then could break free of their parents' lives as farmers. In 1941, Kay Nakao wanted to go to business school. "That's what I really enjoyed: bookkeeping, typing, anything like that," she said in a 1986 oral history. "But the folks figured . . . [I] can't go to college, because they need that extra hand on the farm." In 1945, Nakao and her husband, Sam, did not return to farming, and all three of their children grew up knowing they were expected to attend college. Their two sons, Bruce and Bill, became corporate executives and their daughter, Annie, my classmate and lifelong friend, a teacher.

Because of the new fluidity enjoyed by the young adults and the economic hardships suffered by some older Japanese, Bainbridge lost many of its pioneer families as the camps closed: the Oyamas, the Takayoshis, the Yakawas, the Tonookas, the Nagatanis, the Ohtakis. A perusal of the *Spartan Life* high school yearbooks from the late 1940s and 1950s reflects this. Where once nearly a quarter of the high school was of Japanese descent, after the war only a few Asian faces smile back from class photos.

STUDENT'S MEMBERSHIP CARD
THIS CERTIFIES THAT
Yaeko Sakai
IS A MEMBER OF THE
BAINBRIDGE HIGH SCHOOL
STUDENT'S ASSOCIATION
BOB BELL, Pres.
Non-Transferable   1945-46   No. 130

The returning Islanders, many with young families, became part of day-to-day Bainbridge life soon after settling in. The schools were once again instrumental in easing the transition. Teachers organized August picnics for their students, giving the recently released children the chance to renew friendships before the first day of class.

In 1945 Karen McCormic Beierle was a first grader at the McDonald School in Eagledale, not far from the dock where the *Kehloken* had departed more than three years earlier. In a 2007 interview, Beierle recalled how her mother, Gidsken McCormic, asked her "to be really nice to Frank [Kitamoto] because he's been gone for a long time and is just starting school." Nothing more than that, although Beierle knew instinctively that this was serious. She didn't recall talking later with Kitamoto about that day despite the fact that they became lifelong friends. "He was my date to the Senior Ball, he's been my dentist all these years, and we've just finished working on our fiftieth high school reunion," she said.

McCormic's motherly counsel helped at least one other returning youngster: Wayne Nakata, the five-year-old son of Johnny and Pauline Nakata, whose family had just returned from Moses Lake. When Beierle boarded the old yellow school bus on the first day of school, she found a lone occupant. "[I was] terrified and scared to death," Wayne Nakata recalled in 2007. "She . . . sat next to me, put her arms around me, and said, 'There, there, you're going to make it.'"

Shimako Nishimori Kitano remembered being "quite frightened" as she entered eighth grade that fall, registering under her Americanized middle name, Sally. "I wasn't sure if my former classmates would accept me back," she said. But schoolmates she'd had since kindergarten welcomed her and "the teachers were wonderful and tried to be of help when I began classes."

Excluded families began to return home during the summer of 1945. In order to allow children who had been separated during the years of exclusion to become reacquainted, teachers from schools around the Island organized picnics during August. These picnics became a tradition for years to come. Here, Island students, teachers, and parents gathered in the summer of 1948.

Graduating with Honors

Three events in the 1990s showed the long-lasting significance of World War II and the effect of the Japanese exclusion on Bainbridge Island: two new schools were named for significant players in that struggle, and a long-awaited graduation was held.

In 1992, Bainbridge High School remembered its displaced graduates of 1942. Thirteen young people had been forced to leave their home just weeks before graduation. Fifty years later, these students were invited to participate in the school's formal graduation ceremonies.

Three were able to attend: Sachiko "Sa" Koura Nakata, Nobuko "Nobi" Sakai Omoto, and Sueko "Sue" Nishimori Yonemitsu. Wearing gowns and mortar boards, the women led the procession of graduates. Nakata, who had been a teenaged *Review* reporter at Minidoka, warmly embraced another graduate after receiving her diploma—her grandson Edward Hiroshi Nakata.

Islanders also honored Milly and Walt Woodward on November 5, 1994, as "principal keepers of [the] compass course on the Island in the twentieth century" by naming their new middle school after them. Calling them heroes, school board member Vicki Clayton told the standing-room-only audience at the school's dedication, "They have shown an unwavering commitment to community. In advancing the extraordinary place we call home, they have helped to provide us with the capacity and the will to shape our Island in the future. They have demonstrated the integrity, the quest for excellence, the belief in learning, and the care for others that we seek in the children we educate."

Milly was remembered for her work in planning and shepherding the construction of the Kitsap Regional Library. She was also cited for her campaign in the 1940s to fill or cover abandoned wells that were endangering child safety. Walt's tenure in the 1970s as chair of Washington State's Shorelines Hearings Board was also mentioned.

However, most of the celebration, which began with a barbecue and entertainment by student musicians and athletes and ended with a community dance, centered on the Woodwards' courageous stand fifty years earlier. Joining Clayton in the tribute was Walt and Milly's good friend Junkoh Harui, who in 1942 was a frightened nine-year-old exiled from his home and friends. He shared with the crowd—youngsters and their parents, longtime Islanders and newcomers—his story and how Milly and Walt had affected his life. Many were hearing it for the first time.

Six years later, the school board named the new intermediate school, located just down the road from Woodward Middle School, for Island pioneer Sonoji Sakai. Sakai, with his wife, Yoshiko, and their six children, spent three years behind barbed wire at Manzanar and Minidoka. Shortly after returning to Bainbridge Island, Sonoji sold a large portion of land to the school district at the same price he had paid for it more than a decade earlier. In 1948, the Sakais' strawberry fields became the site of an elementary school and the district offices.

"It's really significant that a person would give up his land, because it was probably the most precious possession he had," Frank Kitamoto told the [Bremerton] *Sun* in 1998. The Sakais' daughter Kay Nakao agreed, saying, "When he sold the land for [the school], I am sure he had some misgivings. It was our livelihood. We grew good berries there."

The Island honored its entire Japanese community at the school's January 9, 2000, dedication. School board member Elaine vonRosentiel said, "We are honoring not only Mr. Sakai but the Bainbridge Island Japanese American community as a whole. . . . We are expressing and memorializing our Island's appreciation for the contributions he and the Bainbridge Japanese American community have made to our cultural, educational, and economic life."

Today, Island schoolchildren learn the story of Sonoji and Yoshiko Sakai. Sakai Intermediate School displays many of the family's treasures, including a doll sent from Japan to young Kay by her grandmother on Girls' Day in 1930—a doll that avoided the destruction of Japanese items during the FBI raids because the family had forgotten that it was packed away in their attic. Nakao's grandmother died in the 1945 bombing of Hiroshima.

Although Walt lived to see the dedication of the school in his and Milly's honor, Milly did not. He noted how the tribute was particularly fitting for Milly, since she had taught school on the Island in the 1930s and again in the 1970s. She would have also appreciated the naming of Sakai School, both as a well-deserved honor to an Island family and the larger Island Japanese American community, and because of its role in educating future Island students about that crucial part of their history.

In 1998, (from left to right) Sakai sisters Yaeko, Nobi, and Kay, along with sister-in-law Kimiko broke ground on the school named in their father's memory, opposite top. Walt and Milly were similarly honored, opposite bottom, when the Island's new middle school was christened in their name. Below: Sa Nakata and grandson Eddie Nakata walked in the 1992 Bainbridge High School graduation ceremony.

While former exiles like Mo (left) and Johnny Nakata, above, who founded Town & Country Market with Ed Loverich, quickly became active community members, the painful memories of the exclusion didn't go away. The healing didn't really begin until the early 1980s, when the film Visible Target, *opposite right, was released. Opposite left: Ethan Schuyler's apology for his father's role in opposing the Nikkei's return.*

Although the Masonic Rainbow Girls denied her membership because of her race, she was warmly embraced by friends like Ray Lowery and Shannon Stafford, who wondered aloud why "Shimako" had become "Sally."

Eiko Suyematsu Shibayama, returning as a sophomore, said that at first "[I] was kind of afraid," but "the neighbor girl that I used to play with came up and welcomed me. She said, 'I'm going to get on the bus with you. I'll take care of you.' And, sure enough, she did." In a 2006 interview, Shibayama did recall an isolated incident of someone yelling "Jap," but "it never happened again."

It wasn't long before the former prisoners were active and productive community members. They became artists, schoolteachers, dentists, florists, and farmers—all important threads in the Island's tapestry. They had become integrated in the way of most immigrants, although perhaps not as quickly.

While Island Issei had mostly kept to themselves, primarily because of the language barrier, their children expanded on friendships formed in the school yard. Decades later, Milly remembered observing that Bainbridge High School "was integrated to quite an extent" in the 1930s and "relations were good between the kids."

Although mixed dating or marriage was not yet happening—at least not openly—they would all be together at high school dances. "They were friends, but they each had their social circles, shall we say."

Mo Nakata began an association with Tom Loverich's son Ed, his friend from high school, working in the grocery located at Bainbridge Gardens. Johnny Nakata was eventually able to buy back the building he had constructed before the war and once again sell groceries at the Eagle Harbor Market in Winslow. In 1957, with the support of a group of local investors, the three grocers—sons of Croatian and Japanese immigrants—joined forces in opening the Island's first supermarket. Today, Town & Country Markets operates stores in five neighboring communities. While Bainbridge Gardens nurtures the Island's soul, "T&C" is surely at its heart, providing much more than merchandise to its many loyal shoppers.

The former exiles stepped quietly back into Island life in countless other ways. One of my special childhood memories is of my Brownie Scout troop, which included friends of varied heritage: Native American, Scandinavian, Yugoslavian, Japanese, British Isles, the Philippines. Our leaders were Mrs. Nakao and Mrs. Hanson. As an adult I've often marveled at the Nikkei's courage to get involved in their community so soon after incarceration, but to us girls in 1954, they were simply two nice ladies—Annie's mom and Marsha's mom.

For decades, the former inmates of Minidoka and Manzanar and the eight other camps did not talk about the exclusion, either among themselves or to their children. "It's almost as if we all got together and agreed [not to discuss it], but of course we didn't," said Kay Nakao in 2007, struggling to explain the Nikkei's silence. "Deep down we wanted to forget it ever happened. Besides, we had to make a living!" With most of their resources gone, many Nikkei took two or more jobs to support their young families. In a quiet voice, the eighty-seven-year-old added, her voice trailing off, "It was such a hurt—the pain . . ."

For the Islanders, the dam burst with the preparation in the early 1980s for *Visible Target*, a PBS documentary about their wartime experience. "Once we started [talking], we couldn't stop," remembered Nakao. Finally, the community began to heal. In 1985 Ethan Schuyler, son of Lambert Schuyler, apologized publicly for his father's role in opposing the return of the Island's Japanese American residents. In an open letter to Islanders published in the *Review,* he wrote, "I wish to apologize and to extend a 'Welcome Home,' even if it is a bit late." Schuyler would later change the spelling of his name to Skyler to distance himself from his father's ideas. Nationally, a public discussion about the history was sparked by a formal apology from the government in 1988. More exiles began to share their stories, and other communities began to heal.

As awareness of the exclusion grew, my parents received much public recognition. However, they were always a little puzzled as to why they should receive such accolades for doing

Film reflects time of painful history

Apologizes for wartime actions

To the Editor:

I would like to publicly apologize for the role my father, Lambert Schuyler, played in making our Americans of Japanese descent feel unwelcome upon their return to their homes on Bainbridge, after being released from military imprisonment during World War II.

In the years following the war, my father regretted his impulsive actions as he came to personally know, respect, and trust many of the imprisoned Americans.

As I look back, I can see that these same gentile people appeared to understand and forgive my father, I have always admired this quality and have applied it many times to my own life.

Clearly, our Americans of Japanese descent are superior citizens and we are lucky to have them as neighbors.

Again, I wish to apologize and to extend a "Welcome Home," even if it is a bit late.

**Ethan Schuyler
Bainbridge Island**

(Bainbridge Review, May 15, 1985)

lots of peaceful fer-
ticking, and scenes
documentary film
focus more sharp-
at some consider
about: "Decem-
ainbridge Island,
oked like the
announcer says.
t, the film pro-
e examination of
he evacuation of
s on Bainbridge

has been in the
of years, is now
air on KCTS-
th.

eration
erican com-
has been in-

The film is also full of the emotions that islanders still feel: Hisa Matsudaira has tears in her eyes as she describes her feelings as a child, Margaret Englund and Rich Barr talk about watching their friends being "kinda herded on the ferry," and many others tell of their experiences in the 1942.

The film does not leave out the feelings of many Americans who felt the evacuation was necessary. Both Eleanor Yost and Carl Pratt talk of the fear of the time after Pearl Harbor.

The film ends with scenes of the island today: Akio Suyematsu's strawberry fields, Frank Kitamoto speaking at a meeting of the Japanese American community, Bainbridge High School classmates at last summer's reunion.

The documentary was not without problems as it was being put together. Funding fell through on one occasion, necessitating a Bain-

VISIBLE TARGET

For years, the shame they felt about the exclusion kept many of the Nikkei from talking about their experiences. But once they began to tell their stories, *opposite,* many realized they could no longer keep silent. Here, Walt and Milly enjoyed a dinner held in their honor at the popular restaurant Ruby Chow's. The Bainbridge Island Nikkei held the event to thank the couple for their years of friendship.

their job. "I feel perpetually amazed," Milly said in 1983. "Every time I turn around there is somebody honoring us, and it's nice but I still can't get used to it. I'm just an ordinary person. I think most people in my shoes would have done the same thing."

In 1963 the Bainbridge Island Japanese community said thank you to Milly and Walt at a dinner in their honor at Ruby Chow's, a popular Chinese restaurant in Seattle. Yoshiaki Amatatsu, representing the Island Nikkei, spoke in Japanese. The Woodwards, he said, "at possible personal sacrifice, stood up in our behalf, which contributed in enabling our return." Further, he attributed the continued success of Island Nikkei to "the deep humanity" of my parents. "Words cannot be found to express the feeling of gratitude in our hearts," he said.

Kay and Sam Nakao, who had become my parents' good friends, shared the head table with them. Sam Nakao and Peter Ohtaki both offered words of thanks and appreciation, and the latter gave Milly and Walt each a gift.

My parents were humbled by the evening: the kind words, the gathering of friends in their honor, the presentation of beautiful watches inscribed with "In Gratitude," and the signing of a moving tribute by nearly 150 people. Milly drew on her university studies as she quietly thanked them with, "*Domo arigato gozaimashita.*"

Respect came from other quarters as well. Their post-war publishing continued to reflect a sentiment they expressed in 1943 after being honored by the Washington State Press Club for "distinguished editorial writing." Walt and Milly had said, "We do not ask our readers to agree with our editorials. But we do feel we are contributing something to our community and, in a small way to America, if our editorials cause our readers to think for themselves."

"They were leaders in the community," said Ralph Munro, retired secretary of state for the state of Washington and a 1961 BHS graduate whose mother taught at Pleasant Beach School in the 1940s. "My dad could get so damn mad at Milly and Walt about certain editorials!" he said in a 2007 interview. Walt was an activist editor, "the kind of guy who loved to poke at things," Munro recalled. "Walt did not write editorials about the sunsets. He wrote about controversial subjects."

Many people assumed those editorials were written exclusively by my father, but Walt liked to set the record straight: "Milly was a modest woman who didn't like to call attention to herself, but you have to credit her with a lot of strength. I never published an editorial without her approval. We were in this together."

They sold the *Bainbridge Review* in 1963 to a local couple. The paper would continue under Island ownership until 1988, when it was bought by a Canadian entrepreneur, ending eighty-eight years of local ownership. As for my

parents, Walt continued as editor of the *Review* until 1965 before returning to his journalistic roots at the *Seattle Times*. Milly also revisited the past when she rejoined the faculty at Bainbridge High School. Walt continued to write occasionally for the *Review* into the 1990s.

In the interim, they raised three daughters: firstborn Carolyn; Mildred, known from infancy as "Mij"; and me. We were all involved in school projects and kept our parents entertained with dance recitals, operettas, speech and debate contests, and myriad other activities. My parents were among the founders of St. Barnabas's Episcopal Church and were lifelong parishioners, and my sisters and I were active in the youth choir and young people's group. My parents also enjoyed attending local cultural events, with Walt clapping his hands above his head for a good performance.

The highlight of each year for the Woodward family was August when, aboard a succession of three progressively larger *Big Toot*s, we gloried in the idyllic near-isolation of a lovely spot in the San Juan Islands, just off the Straits of Georgia, which separate the U.S. from Canada. Now a state park, tiny Matia Island was an undiscovered gem in the 1950s. We often spent the entire month without seeing another person, except perhaps the young charges from a nearby YMCA camp, whose counselors became much more interesting as we sisters got older. We fished for salmon, shucked oysters, played very competitive Hearts and Double Solitaire, and scrambled over moss-covered rocks to find the elusive Indian paintbrush. After we daughters were grown, our parents continued cruising, eventually navigating the Inside Passage to Alaska and returning to Juneau in *Big Toot III*.

Milly somehow balanced her duties at the *Review* with being there for us when the school bus dropped us off. She also found time to serve on the boards of the Totem Girl Scout Council and the Kitsap County Library, and work with the Kitsap County Court as it developed improved juvenile facilities. She participated in the Bainbridge Island Choristers and several amateur theatrical performances. She was a devoted gardener and, like many Islanders at the time, fed her roses with salmon carcasses and the occasional dogfish, seeking advice from nurseryman Junkoh Harui. When it came to groceries, her loyalty never faltered: she followed Johnny Nakata from his Eagle Harbor Grocery to the shiny new T&C when it opened in 1957.

After they sold the Review *in 1963, Milly, opposite top, returned to teaching at Bainbridge High School, and Walt, opposite bottom, to the* Seattle Times. *Above: Milly and Walt in British Columbia, aboard* Big Toot II. *The Woodwards sailed to points around the Pacific Northwest with daughters, below (from top to bottom), Mary, Mildred (known as "Mij"), and Carolyn, and later during their retirement.*

During the 1950s and early 1960s, the school yard was once again significant in unifying the Island's younger generation. Just three when his family was exiled during the war, Hiroshi "Hiro" Hayashida was a high school student in the 1950s. As teenagers do, he spent many afternoons and evenings at his best friend's house. His best friend? Lambert Schuyler's older son, Lambert Jr. A few years later, I became friends with Schuyler's younger son, Ethan, and we dated for a while. How odd both of those friendships must have seemed to Islanders with long memories! To the credit of all three sets of parents, nothing of past rancor was shared with us teenagers. Hiro and Lambert Jr., and Ethan and I remain good friends.

My father managed the campaigns of Catherine May when she was elected to Congress in 1958, and Lloyd Andrews, who was narrowly defeated by Governor Albert D. Rosellini in his reelection bid in 1960. Walt was a columnist and a member of the *Seattle Times*'s editorial board from 1966 to 1977. He wrote frequently on boating and subsequently published two books on the subject. Governor Daniel J. Evans appointed him as the first chair of the state's Pollution Control Hearings Board in the 1970s. A concerned environmentalist, Walt also became the first hearings examiner for the state's Shorelines

Walt, who wrote a boating column for the Seattle Times, taught boating safety, and was a Commodore in the Poulsbo Yacht Club. Here, he and Milly are seen aboard Big Toot II in the 1960s. They were happiest in their later years when sailing aboard one of their boats. In 1982, the couple sailed their newest boat, Big Toot III, through the Inside Passage to Juneau, Alaska, where they first met in 1934.

Hearings Board. Locally, he served as the Island's first land use hearings examiner. He was among one hundred citizens inducted into Washington State's "Centennial Hall of Fame" in 1989.

In 1985, their wartime story was told in the PBS documentary *Visible Target* by producers John de Graaf and Cris Anderson, based on extensive interviews of Islanders recalling the events of 1941 to 1945. The project took its name from a comment by Sam Nakao: "There were many people who [supported us], but very few . . . came out front and became a visible target like [the Woodwards] did."

In 1986, my parents were grand marshals in Bainbridge Island's Grand Old Fourth parade. They were surprised when the parade was interrupted as Art Koura presented an American flag and a certificate of appreciation "for your outstanding courage" from the veterans of the 100th Infantry Battalion, the 442nd Regimental Combat Team, and the Military Intelligence Service. Koura said, "You had the insight and the faith in our form of government, and even more, the courage to speak out when unpopular to do so. No American can do more for his country."

Other honors were given to them for their stand on constitutional rights. The Kitsap County Bar Association honored them on Law Day in 1986 with the Liberty Bell Award for "[holding] before this community the reality of the law . . . [when] the U.S. Supreme Court forgot that we were a nation ruled by law."

They were also honored by the people whose constitutional rights had been violated. The national Japanese American Citizens League presented Walt and Milly with the first-ever Edison Uno Memorial Civil Rights Award, named for a San Francisco State University professor known for his passion for justice. Paul Ohtaki, now of San Francisco and ever dear to my parents' hearts, joined them at the 1986 event in Chicago.

At the second Manzanar reunion in 1987, former inmates declared the Woodwards "Defenders of the Constitution" and presented them with an extraordinary artistic interpretation of the camp by Mary Ichiro. Kay and Sam Nakao shared the journey to California with Milly and Walt.

Throughout their lives, my parents were enthusiastic supporters of community activities, especially involving youth. One local wit, reflecting on their quarter-century association with the *Bainbridge Review,* observed, "They survived three office moves, two fires, and tens of thousands of parents looking for their child's name in print." A BHS classmate of mine, author Pat Dillon, a columnist and later an editor with the San Jose *Mercury News,* summed up what Walt and Milly meant to Bainbridge Island: "Week in and week out, the Woodwards got our names right, our events, the Little League scores and standings, the school bus schedules and lunch menus, the tide schedules, the direction of the economic, social, and political winds. They got them right and even raised hell doing it." Remembering both the exclusion and a hard-fought battle against a bridge linking Bainbridge and Seattle, Dillon wrote, "They fought off a governor and business interests" in support of the Island.

In 2003 my parents were honored posthumously at the Minidoka reunion "for believing in the Constitution and for championing the rights of the Nikkei."

That same year, at the first national Kansha Awards in 2003, the National Japanese American Historical Society honored my parents, four other non-Nikkei individuals, and one group—the American Friends Service Committee—for their courage and kindness during the exclusion. ("Kansha" in Japanese means "in gratitude.") Milly and Walt were also honored by fellow journalists. The Washington Newspaper Publishers' Association in 1998 presented Walt with its Freedom's Light Award. In 2001, both the Society of Professional Journalists and the Asian American Journalists Association honored them for their journalistic integrity.

My parents never thought of themselves as heroes. As Frank Kitamoto recalled, "When Walt went out to schools with me to talk to students, we'd

Walt, shown above with the Edison Uno Memorial Civil Rights Award, was recognized along with Milly with a series of honors including the Liberty Bell Award, below, and a certificate of appreciation, opposite, from members of the 100th Infantry Battalion, the 442nd, and the MIS. Opposite top: Walt as grand marshal of Bainbridge's Fourth of July Parade in the late 1990s with grandsons Brodie (left) and Riley.

Nidoto Nai Yoni– Let It Not Happen Again

The entire Bainbridge Island community regularly comes together in recognition of the exclusion, both out of respect for its exiled neighbors and in hopes it will never happen again. When the Islanders departed in 1942, it was overcast and drizzling. Sixty years later on March 30, 2002, under similarly cool and overcast skies, more than five hundred people gathered at the departure site to dedicate a memorial "to honor those who suffered and to cherish their friends and community who stood by them and welcomed them home." The beat of taiko drums echoed across the water. Wearing I.D. tags reminiscent of those attached to people and luggage in 1942, the crowd, undeterred by the threatening skies, listened as Governor Gary Locke, U.S. Representative Jay Inslee, and other officials spoke.

Locals, some of whom had experienced the exclusion, also spoke. The affable Jerry Nakata, unable to attend because of ill health, was there in spirit as two of his old high school buddies–Hal Champeness and Earl Hanson–told the rapt group how devastating it was to watch their irrepressible pal marched off the Island and out of their young lives.

Emily Groff, accompanying herself on the guitar, gave a haunting acoustic rendition of "Don't Fence Me In," a song popularized by Bing Crosby in the 1940s. Then the names of all 227 exiled Bainbridge Islanders were read, clearly and respectfully, by three young *sansei*– third-generation Nikkei. As the sun broke through the clouds, the ceremony closed as all joined in singing "America, the Beautiful."

Finally the memorial, set in a four-foot-tall granite stone under a weeping cedar tree amid hellebores and moss, was revealed as friends, both new and lifelong, read the words of remembrance and healing. More than a few shed tears.

Five years later on the sixty-fifth anniversary in 2007, much was the same–the taiko drummers, Groff's evocative song, the solemn list of names, dignitaries and local folk sharing their thoughts. Once again, it threatened rain. Two bald eagles, national symbols of freedom and liberty, circled overhead.

Those attending in 2007 also got their first look at what the community hopes will become part of the National Park Service's Minidoka National Monument. Working in partnership with three local agencies–the City of Bainbridge Island, the local parks department, and the Bainbridge Island Historical Society–the small memorial committee has made great strides toward the goal of creating a memorial park on the site of the former dock where the Island Nikkei

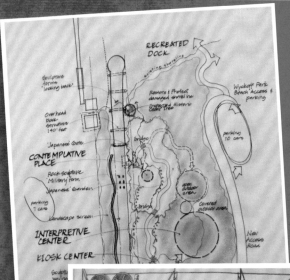

departed for the camps. Enthusiastic support, both monetary and otherwise, continues to come from the community and from the government at every level.

Committee member Lilly Kitamoto Kodama, who was seven years old in 1942, commented on the strong local involvement of individuals. "It couldn't have started without the support of the greater community," she told a local reporter in 2007. "That's what's so meaningful."

Nationally renowned Island architect Johnpaul Jones, whose projects include Seattle's Children's Museum and the National Museum of the American Indian in Washington, D.C., has worked with the committee from its inception, donating many hours of his time for the memorial. His designs interpret the community's concepts with sensitivity and beauty. A "Memorial Wall" is the central feature that gracefully honors those who endured the exclusion.

After nine years of local work toward a memorial, the House of Representatives voted unanimously in 2007 to extend federal status to the project. In 2008 the Senate added its approval and President George W. Bush signed it into law. With federal support, Islanders will begin to work with the National Park Service to show where it all began, as well as tell of Bainbridge Island's unique support of its exiles.

When completed, the memorial will include an interpretive center designed to inform visitors on all aspects of the exclusion in hopes it will fulfill its name, *Nidoto Nai Yoni*—Let It Not Happen Again. Inslee, who has backed the project from the outset, said, "We don't sit in judgment of the past, but in inspiration for the future."

Fumiko Nishinaka Hayashida, the mother of Leonard—the first Island child born at Manzanar—is a spirited proponent of the memorial. At ninety-six and as the oldest Bainbridge survivor of the camps, she traveled to Washington, D.C., a month before the sixty-fifth anniversary to give congressional testimony in support of the memorial bill. Hayashida was surprised and hopeful at the change in attitude toward the incarceration that she has seen over the past sixty-five years. "I thought nobody cared. I'm very happy. I hope I live to see it done."

In 2002, a memorial, shown below with BIJAC president Frank Kitamoto, was dedicated to Islanders who were exiled and the community members who supported them. The memorial is located on the site where Island Nikkei were transported off the Island en route to Manzanar. Opposite: Early plans for the memorial, which will become a satellite unit of the Minidoka National Internment Monument in 2008.

While they never thought of themselves as such, Walt and Milly, opposite top at the second Manzanar reunion, were heroes to those whom they defended. The Nikkei showed their gratitude by presenting them with Mary Ichiro's artistic interpretation of the camp, seen here. Opposite bottom: A Special Recognition Award given to the couple by the Asian American Journalist Association for their journalistic integrity.

have some long conversations in the car getting there. One day, Walt said to me, 'I don't know why Milly and I are getting all these awards and recognition. We just did what we thought was right. You people are the real heroes. You should be getting the awards and recognition. The story is about you.' I thought to myself, Wow, here is a really special man. He didn't think of himself as another 'shining white knight in armor' riding to our rescue and playing the lead in our 'movie.' He really is a special hero."

Other Islanders—*many* other Islanders—were also friends and defenders of their Nikkei neighbors, and didn't think of themselves as heroes, either. But of course they are. Just as Walt and Milly are. Too many names of the Islanders who stored a family's china, or cared for a pet, or made a point to check on a neighbor's house have been lost. But what they did is evident on Bainbridge Island today. And their efforts are remembered in the hearts of those they helped.

With no public recognition and never any payment, many former exiles said "thank you" by unobtrusively assisting these neighbors who had eased their wartime plight. Clark Burkheimer, namesake of his grandfather, recalled in 2007: "Every Saturday after working all week as a checker at T&C, Kay Nakao would come to my grandmother's and clean her house." Burkheimer also recounted how Tad Sakuma, by the 1950s a much sought-after local gardener, faithfully appeared every week to mow his grandparents' lawn. These are but two examples of how Islanders expressed their gratitude to neighbors for their generosity and friendship at a time when so many others had forsaken them.

My parents never forgot the many other people who supported their neighbors. After Art Koura's Fourth of July presentation, my father wrote,

> You see, when American citizens of Japanese ancestry did return to their homes, many of them had to face flaming crosses at night, burned barns and ugly "No Japs Wanted Here" signs. None of that occurred on Bainbridge Island. Our Nisei came home to quiet welcomes and, as we all know, now are respected and integrated members of our community. So that certificate—and the American flag—belong to all our fellow Islanders.

On the sixty-sixth anniversary of their removal, Shig Moritani (center) and Kay Nakao, along with Earl Hanson, admired the work of local timber framers who donated their time to erect the first buildings of the planned memorial on the former site of the Eagledale Dock. Nakao and Hanson were present at the dedication of the site in 2004. For Moritani, this was the first time he had returned since March 30, 1942.

From the moment they first met in 1934 to their fiftieth wedding anniversary in 1985, above, and right up to Milly's death in 1989, Walt and Milly were inseparable. The love they shared filled their lives and heartened those around them, as was evident in the many tributes to them after their deaths, opposite below. Opposite above: Portraits of the couple that hang in the school named in their honor.

In 1941, my parents had "thrown [their] permanent lot with Bainbridge Island." For most of their tenure at the *Bainbridge Review*, it really was "the only newspaper in the world that cared about Bainbridge Island." Their former colleague and longtime friend and fellow boater, Wayne Jacobi, explained that "the Island (it was always capitalized in The Review) was the center of the earth, and maybe the universe. The only people who mattered were Islanders. The only stories that made the paper were those dealing with Island issues or Island people."

Milly and Walt were certainly aware of the national impact the forced exile had on almost 120,000 Japanese Americans from the West Coast. However, their focus was on the fewer than three hundred Islanders who were affected. Much of what my parents did during the war was to smooth the way home for those few.

My mother died in 1989 after a difficult, fourteen-year struggle with Parkinson's disease. In 1995 author David Guterson was awarded the PEN/Faulkner Award for *Snow Falling on Cedars,* an intricate, sensitive story that has its roots in the exclusion of Japanese Americans from the Puget Sound area. The novel, in which editor Arthur Chambers is patterned after my father, was made into a movie in 1999. My father died in 2001. At his memorial, the usually reticent Guterson acknowledged a debt of gratitude to my father and observed that, after sixty years, Walt "is still inspiring us all to be as decent and good and fair as we can be."

Hundreds attended my parents' memorials, some traveling thousands of miles. Many others, including a significant number who had never met either of them, wrote of the impact Walt and Milly had on their lives. Both of their deaths were covered in detail by newspapers and electronic media throughout Washington, along the Pacific Coast, and in Japan.

At my father's memorial in 2001, former state official Ralph Munro reminded the guests of one of Thomas Jefferson's pithy comments: "Were it left to me to decide whether we should have a government without newspapers, or newspapers without government, I should not hesitate a moment to prefer the latter." Munro praised my parents' consistent dedication to principles, saying, "The light of liberty never flickered in their hands."

In 1941 Milly and Walt had declared, "We seek the Island's friendship and support, for we intend to make The Review our life's work." They appreciated and were humbled by each of the many recognitions that came as a result of their work, but none meant more than the dinner in 1963 at Ruby Chow's, when they were surrounded by a roomful of Island neighbors—their friends. As they shared that evening with friends, my parents had no doubt their life's work, although far from over, had been of value.

Nearly forty years later, my father's memorial, held in the gymnasium of Woodward Middle School, was in many ways a celebration of both his and Milly's lives. Suzanne Downing, the *Review* editor in the early 1990s, reflected on the continuing influence of two editors from "all those years ago" and cogently observed, "[Walt] and Milly both believed in community and knew that a newspaper is a connector that ties the community together." They had spent their lives, in Downing's words, giving "a voice to people who had no voice . . . the Garden Club, the libraries, the schools, the kids," thereby bringing their beloved Island together. It was a fitting farewell to a couple whose lives had been dedicated to honest reporting and who "always [strove] to speak the truth, unafraid, whether it be on a national issue or something purely local."

6 THE SEATTLE TIMES **OPINION** FRIDAY, MARCH 16, 2001

EDITORIALS
THE NEWSPAPER'S VIEW

Walter C. Woodward smiles after receiving the Freedom's Light award from the Washington Newspaper Publishers Association in 1998.

HANK WONG / THE SEATTLE TIMES

QUIET, PERSISTENT COURAGE

MEMORIAL services for Walter C. Woodward, whose editorials in the Bainbridge Review decried the internment of Japanese Americans at the onset of World War II, will be held in the island church he helped found.

Woodward, who died Tuesday at 91, bought the Bainbridge Island newspaper with his wife Mildred in 1940.

Their courageous path was foreshadowed in a special edition published Dec. 7, 1941, that noted editorially:

"If ever a community was devastated by events over which it had no control, it is Bainbridge Island this day and we dare not forget our neighbors of Japanese ancestry."

Three hundred angry people turned out to a community meeting to run the young couple out of town.

Eventually, the local protests ran out of steam, but the co-editors never lost their passionate belief that a grave constitutional wrong had been inflicted by infamous Executive Order 9066, which led to the forced departure and internment of Japanese Americans.

The Woodwards would not go. Alone on the West Coast, their editorial voice hammered away at the injustice. Advertising revenues and circulation suffered, but the couple

THIS WEEK

Mildred Woodward

✔ Milly Woodward, former co-publisher of the Bainbridge Review, died Saturday at her Winslow home after suffering from Parkinson's disease for 14 years. She was recognized nationally for the editorial stand she took during World War II in strenuous opposition to the wartime internment of American citizens of Japanese ancestry. An obituary written by her husband is on page A13.

Index

Quotation Source Notes

AI = author interview. BI = BIJAC interview. BR = *Bainbridge Review*. DP = Densho Project interview. VT = *Visible Target* interview (1983). PJD = *Personal Justice Denied*. PTI = *Paper Trail to Internment* by James Watanabe. PWT = *Prisoners Without Trial*. SPI = *Seattle Post-Intelligencer*. WWM = Walt Woodward memorial (3/24/2001).

Amatatsu, Yoshiaki: Translation of 1963 speech. American Civil Liberties Union: Summer 1980 *Perspectives: The Civil Rights Quarterly*. Anson, Austin: 5/9/1942 *Saturday Evening Post*. Axelrod, Dee: 2005 BR supplement "Bainbridge Island Almanac." Barr, Rich: VT. Beierle, Karen McCormic: 2007 AI. Berry, Angela: 2007 BI; 1998 self-published history of Felix Narte, Sr., "Island Grown." Biddle, Francis: PJD. Bissell, Clayton: 9/29/1945 remarks at MIS graduation ceremony as quoted in MacNaughton, James C., *Nisei Linguist*. Burkheimer, Clark: 2007 AI. Clayton, Vicki: 11/15/1994 program notes from dedication of Woodward Middle School. Corpuz, Gina: 2007 BI. Daniels, Rogers: PWT. DeWitt, John L.: Summer 1980 *Perspectives: The Civil Rights Quarterly*; 12/26/1941 telephone conversation quoted on the Virtual Museum of the City of San Francisco (sfmuseum.org); PJD; "Resisting Arrest," Salon.com, 2/29/2008. Dillon, Patrick: 9/13/1988, 10/18/1988, and 8/21/1989 *San Jose Mercury News* columns. Downing, Suzanne: WWM. Durrell, Gordon: 3/38/2007 BR. Englund, Margaret: VT. Ford, Leland: PJD. Guterson, David: WWM. Hanson, Earl: 2007 AI; 2007 BI; 2004 DP. Harui, Junkoh: 2007 AI; 2007 BI; 1998 DP; VT. Hayashida, Fumiko: 2007 and 2008 AI; 3/31/2007 SPI; 2006 BI; 1998 DP. Hoover, J. Edgar: PJD. Ikeda, Thomas: 2007 email to author. Irons, Peter: letter to Fred Korematsu quoted by Dale Ikeda, "The Japanese American Story of Internment and Redress," 4/7/2004. Jacobi, Wayne: 2006 and 2007 AI; 3/21/2001 BR. Inslee, Jay: 3/30/2007 remarks for sixty-fifth anniversary of Island exclusion at Nidoto Nai Yoni memorial. Kitamoto, Frank: 2002 BI; 7/30/1998 *Bremerton Sun* article. Kitamoto, Shigeko: 1987 BI; VT. Kitano, Shimako: 2006 AI; two unpublished essays. Knox, Frank: PJD. Kodama, Lilly: 3/31/2007 SPI. Korematsu, Fred: 1999 transcript from *Of Civil Wrongs & Rights: The Fred Korematsu Story*. Koura, Arthur: 1986 and 2002 BI; 7/9/1986 BR; VT. Koura, Hatsuko: 1988 BI. Koura, Noboru: 1987 and 2002 BI; VT. Langlie,

Arthur B.: PTI. Lippmann, Walter: 2/12/1942 *New York Herald Tribune* syndicated column; 2/16/1942 *Washington Post* syndicated column. *Los Angeles Times*: PWT. Loverich, Gary: 2007 AI. MacArthur, Douglas: *A Celebration of Hope and Healing*, Nisei Veterans Committee, 2000. Magnuson, Warren G.: 4/29/1945 SPI. Matsudaira, Hisako: 1988 and 2002 BI; VT. McLemore, Henry: 1/30/1942 *Seattle Times* syndicated column. Merrill, Frank: *Honor by Fire* by Lyn Crost. Milliken, Earl: PTI. Moritani, Tatsukichi: 1987 and 2006 BI. Munro, Ralph: 2007 AI; WWM. Murrow, Edward R.: PWT. Nagatani, Ichiro: VT; 10/30/1981 letter to Commission on Wartime Relocation; 10/30/1981 letter to Japanese American Citizens League. Nakao, Isami: 1987 and 1988 BI; VT. Nakao, Kazuko: 2005, 2006, 2007, and 2008 AI; 1986 and 2006 BI; 7/30/1998 *Bremerton Sun* article; VT. Nakata, Gerald: 2005, 2006, and 2007 AI; 2006 BI; 2006 DP. Nakata, Sachiko: VT. Nakata, Wayne: 2007 AI. Ohtaki, Paul: 2005, 2006, 2007, and 2008 AI; self-published reproduction of scrapbook, "It Was the Right Thing to Do." Omoto, Nobuko: 2007 AI; 2006 BI; VT. Omoto, Setsuo: 1991 transcript of speech to Bainbridge High School class of 1941. Omoto, Yukiko Kitayama: 2007 AI. Pegler, Westbrook: PJD. Rankin, John E.: 12/15/1941 Congressional Record 77th Cong., 2nd session. Rapada, Doreen Almazan: 2007 BI. Roosevelt, Franklin D.: 8/30/1925 *Macon Telegraph*; 1936 order for surveillance of Nikkei in Hawaii as cited on dneiwert.blogspot.com 2/15/2003. Sakai, Toshio: 1975 BI. *San Francisco Chronicle*: 11/8/1941 and 2/1/1942 editorials. Shibayama, Eiko: 2006 BI. Shibayama, Zenji: 2006 BI. Umezuka, Chiye Shigamura: 1980 BI. Takayoshi, Henry: 1988 BI. Truman, Harry S.: *Honor by Fire*. Unnamed Bellevue woman: 2/14/1992 unpublished article by Peggy Reynolds. vonRosentiel, Elaine: 1/9/2000 program notes from dedication of Sonoji Sakai Intermediate School. Wallgren, Mon C.: 1/23/1945 SPI. Warren, Earl: *Congress, Civil Liberties, and the War on Terrorism* by Neal Devins. Watanabe, Ikuko Amatatsu: 2007 AI; 2007 BI. Willoughby, Charles: *A Celebration of Hope*. Woodward, Mildred Logg: VT. Woodward, Walter: 1994 video *Bainbridge: Voices of an Island*; VT. Yamashita, Masaharu: 1987 BI. Yost, Elinor: 1960 conversation as recounted by Mij Woodward; VT.

About the Author & Suggested Reading

A graduate in history from Whitman College and former history teacher, Mary Woodward is the daughter of the late Walt and Milly Woodward. She is a frequent lecturer and columnist on the history and politics of the exclusion, is active in the preservation of Bainbridge Island history, and has been a leader in the creation of the Bainbridge Island Nikkei WWII Internment and Exclusion Memorial. She lives on Bainbridge Island.

This book, while not intended as a definitive study of the exclusion, is firmly rooted in the more extensive works of respected scholars. Equally important are oral histories of and interviews with local residents, both Nikkei and otherwise.

Two collections of contemporary *Bainbridge Review* articles by Paul Ohtaki and Sa Nakata, the first and last "staff correspondents," are available for study at the Bainbridge Island Historical Society (BIHS). Ohtaki's includes articles and letters through Walt Woodward's death in 2001.

Both BIHS and the University of Washington have exclusion archives, many of which are available online.

The Bainbridge Island Japanese American Community (BIJAC) continues to record oral histories of its members, working in concert with the Densho Project (Densho.com), a stellar Seattle non-profit dedicated to providing online information telling the Nikkei's story through a remarkable and growing collection.

Visible Target, *After Silence*, and *Bainbridge: Voices of an Island* are three helpful videos. Local videographers Lucy Ostrander and Don Sellers have prepared several DVDs focusing on different aspects of the Island's exclusion story for IslandWood's Cultural History Series.

Two books provide comparative local studies of the exclusion:

Flewelling, Stan, *Shirakawa: Stories from a Pacific Northwest Japanese American Community*. Auburn: White River Valley Museum, 2002.

Neiwert, David A., *Strawberry Days: How Internment Destroyed a Japanese American Community*. New York: Palgrave MacMillan, 2005.

A standard resource in telling the story of the immigrants' early years on Bainbridge Island:

Price, Andrew, Jr., *Port Blakely: The Community Captain Renton Built*. Reprint, Bainbridge Island: BIHS, 2005.

To tell Bainbridge Island's story, it is necessary to orient it within the larger national picture. Six books, all well respected by scholars in the field, are particularly valuable. When referring to these works, it is helpful to pay particular attention to their bibliographies and endnotes, which offer suggestions for further research. These include:

Commission on Wartime Relocation of Internment of Civilians, *Personal Justice Denied*. Reprint Seattle: University of Washington Press, 1996.

Daniels, Roger, *Prisoners Without Trial: Japanese Americans in World War II*. New York: Hill and Wang, revised edition, 2004. Daniels has many other books worthy of attention.

Fisher, Anne Reeploeg, *Exile of a Race*. Seattle: F. & T. Publishers, 1965.

Kashima, Tetsuden, *Judgment Without Trial: Japanese American Imprisonment During World War II*. Seattle: University of Washington Press, 2003.

Robinson, Greg, *By Order of the President: FDR and the Internment of Japanese Americans*. Cambridge: Harvard University Press, 2001.

Weglyn, Michi, *Years of Infamy: The Untold Story of America's Concentration Camps*. Reprint Seattle: University of Washington Press, 1996.

A final note: the Internet is a treasure trove of information on this topic, but beware and always verify what you find there against the work of serious scholars whose reputations speak to the validity of their work.

Photography Credits

Bainbridge Island Historical Society: 32–33, 34, 35 (object), 42, 43, 49 (object), 84, 85, 143 (photographs)

Bainbridge Island Historical Society, George Munro Family Collection: 56 (object), 59, and back cover (upper object)

Bainbridge Island Historical Society, donated by Kazuko "Kay" Nakao: 48 and back cover (lower object)

Bainbridge Island Historical Society, R. F. Skinner Collection: 50–51

Bainbridge Island Historical Society, Bill Weld Collection: 44, 45, 100, 101 (upper)

Courtesy of Bainbridge Island Japanese American Community: 2–3, 75, 94 (lower), 136

Courtesy of Bainbridge Island Japanese American Community, Nagatani & Moritani Collections: 31 (objects), 62 (objects), 87 (object), 94 (upper), 98

© Keith Brofsky Photography: 8–9, 119, 140–141

Courtesy of Gerald Elfendahl: 108–109, 130, 131 (upper), 132–133, 134 (upper)

Courtesy of Junkoh Harui: 31 (upper), 53, 118

Courtesy of Fusako Horishige: 47

Courtesy of Phyllis Nagatani Kagawa: 68 (object)

Courtesy of Frank Kitamoto: 64, 92 (upper), 96 (upper), 124 (upper), 125, 137

Courtesy of Lilly Kodama: 89, 121 (upper)

Courtesy of Mary Koura: 35 (upper), 77 (upper)

© Ryan Kozu: Author portrait

Library of Congress, Prints & Photographs Division: 6–7, 63, 74, 113

Courtesy of Gary Loverich: 29

Courtesy of Hisa Matsudaira: 90–91, 92 (object), 95, 122–123

Courtesy of Kazuko Nakao: 46 (lower), 57, 97, 99, 127 (right), 129

Courtesy of Larry Nakata: 46 (upper), 102, 110, 126, 135 (upper)

Courtesy of Ron Nakata: 77 (object), 93, 96 (object), 101 (objects), 105, 107, 112, 114 (objects), 115

Courtesy of Yoshi Nakata: 120

National Archives: 7–8, 76, 82–83

Courtesy of Paul Ohtaki: 54, 55, 67, 86

Courtesy of Robert Oliver: 22–23

Courtesy of Nobuko Sakai Omoto; 14, 38, 80, 103, 114 (upper), 117, 127 (left), 131 (lower), 143 (objects)

Courtesy of Yuki Omoto: 72–73, and dust jacket flap (upper)

Courtesy of Puget Sound Maritime Historical Society: 30

Seattle Post-Intelligencer Collection, Museum of History & Industry, Seattle: 4–5, 12, 40–41, 49 (upper), 56 (upper), 58, 60–61, 62 (upper), 65, 68 (upper), 69, 70, 71, 106 (upper), back cover (upper) and front cover (lower)

Theodore Geisel Collection, University of California, San Diego: 79

Courtesy of Carolyn Woodward: 16, 37, 39, 142

Courtesy of Mary Woodward: 18, 19, 20, 21, 24, 25, 26, 27, 36, 37 (lower), 52, 104, 106 (object), 111, 124 (object), 128, 134 (object), 135 (object), 138, 139, dust jacket flap (lower), back cover (lower), and front cover (upper)

Courtesy of Yae Yoshihara: 81, 87, 121 (object)

All photographs of archival prints, documents, and objects were taken by Fenwick Publishing.

Acknowledgments

Karen Beierle

Paul and Debbi Brainerd

Clark Burkheimer

Kate Carruthers

Ralph Cheadle

Douglas Crist

Steve and Harriet Davis

Mark Dawson

Robert and Noriko Dozono

Patrick and Susan Dunn

Hank and Tomi Egashira

Sherri Egashira

Gerald Elfendahl

MaryAnn Faubion Kohl

Ellen Ferguson

Hugh and Jane Ferguson Foundation

Roy and Mary Garrett

Dave Goller

Debra Grindeland

David Guterson

Rhea Hannon

Earl Hanson

Fumi Hayashida

Elizabeth Helbig Grossman

Tom Ikeda

Roger Ishihara

John Ishizuka

Wayne Jacobi

Marc and Hajni Joslun

Tetsuden Kashima

Neil King

Dr. Walter and May Kitagawa

Frank Kitamoto

Ted Kitayama

Joe and Lilly Kodama

J.C. and Sheridan Ley-Mackey

Gary Loverich

Alissa Lynch

Mike and Linda MacDowell

The Mahjongettes

George Marishita

Hisa Matsudaira

Jim Matsudaira

Gidsken McCormic

Tomio Moriguchi

Shig Moritani

Ralph and Karen Munro

Richard Myers

Mas Nagami

Mako Nakagawa

Kay Nakao

Jerry Nakata

Kathy, Rick, Jerry, Yuka, & Kristi Nakata

Larry Nakata

Wayne Nakata

Paul Ohtaki

Nobi Omoto

Yuki Omoto

Joan Piper

Gene Priestman and Susan Guffey

Quail Roost Foundation

Dana Quitslund

Nancy Quitslund

Chris Reiter

Gary Sakuma

Lorraine Scott

Grace Shibayama

Suquamish Tribal Council

Jack Swanson

Stephanie Toothman

Town & Country Markets

Wakimoto Charitable Foundation

Janet Westbrook-Gardner

Carol and Sandy White

Barbara Winther

Carolyn Woodward

Mij Woodward

Brodie Woodward-Pratt

Riley Woodward-Pratt

Yae Yoshihara

Anonymous